Readings for Writers

Pueblo Community College

English 121: English Composition I

CCR 094: College Composition and Reading

Bedford/St. Martin's   BOSTON ◆ NEW YORK

Manufactured in the United States of America.

For information, write: Bedford/St. Martin's, 75 Arlington Street, Boston, MA 02116 (617-399-4000)

Contents

iii

Evaluation

Argument

CONTENTS

TAYLOR CLARK

Meatless Like Me

A Pacific Northwest native, **Taylor Clark** is a journalist and freelance writer based in Portland, Oregon. Since his graduation from Dartmouth College in 2002, Clark has written for a variety of publications, including *GQ* and *Psychology Today*, and served as a staff writer for *Williamette Week*, Portland's alternative weekly newspaper. During his time at *Williamette Week*, he reported on local government, personalities, and popular culture. His books include *Starbucked: A Double Tall Tale of Caffeine, Commerce, and Culture* (2007), which chronicles Starbucks's expansion into and domination of the global coffee market, and *Nerve: Poise under Pressure, Serenity under Stress, and the Brave New Science of Fear and Cool* (2011).

In "Meatless Like Me," Clark addresses his omnivorous readers, explaining, in an attempt to debunk the stereotypes and misconceptions associated with vegetarianism, why he chooses not to eat meat. In his characteristic style, Clark uses humor as he attempts to foster mutual understanding between skeptical omnivores and his fellow herbivores.

Every vegetarian remembers his first time. Not the unremarkable event of his first meal without meat, mind you. No, I mean the first time he casually lets slip that he's turned herbivore, prompting everyone in earshot to stare at him as if he just revealed plans to sail his carrot-powered plasma yacht to Neptune. For me, this first time came at an Elks scholarship luncheon in rural Oregon when I was 18. All day, I'd succeeded at seeming a promising and responsible young man, until that fateful moment when someone asked why I hadn't taken any meat from the buffet. After I offered my reluctant explanation—and the guy announced it *to the entire room*—30 people went eerily quiet, undoubtedly expecting me to launch into a speech on the virtues of hemp. In the corner, an elderly, suited man glared at me as he slowly raised a slice of bologna and executed the most menacing bite of cold cut in recorded history. I didn't get the scholarship.

Taylor Clark, "Meatless Like Me." From *Slate.com*, posted May 7, 2008, 11:51 AM, EST. Used by permission of Slate.com.

1

I tell this story not to win your pity but to illustrate a point: I've been vegetarian for a decade, and when it comes up, I still get a look of confused horror that says, "But you seemed so . . . *normal.*" The U.S. boasts more than 10 million herbivores today, yet most Americans assume that every last one is a loopy, self-satisfied health fanatic, hellbent on draining all the joy out of life. Those of us who want to avoid the social nightmare have to hide our vegetarianism like an Oxycontin addiction, because admit it, omnivores: You know nothing about us. Do we eat fish? Will we panic if confronted with a hamburger? Are we dying of malnutrition? You have no clue. So read on, my flesh-eating friends — I believe it's high time we cleared a few things up.

To demonstrate what a vegetarian really is, let's begin with a simple thought experiment. Imagine a completely normal person with completely normal food cravings, someone who has a broad range of friends, enjoys a good time, is carbon-based, and so on. Now remove from this person's diet anything that once had eyes, and, *wham!*, you have yourself a vegetarian. Normal person, no previously ocular food, end of story. Some people call themselves vegetarians and still eat chicken or fish, but unless we're talking about the kind of salmon that comes freshly plucked from the vine, this makes you an omnivore. A select few herbivores go one step further and avoid *all* animal products — milk, eggs, honey, leather — and they call themselves *vegan*, which rhymes with "tree men." These people are intense.

Vegetarians give up meat for a variety of ethical, environmental, and health reasons that are secondary to this essay's goal of increasing brotherly understanding, so I'll mostly set them aside. Suffice it to say that one day, I suddenly realized that I could never look a cow in the eyes, press a knocking gun to her temple, and pull the trigger without feeling I'd done something cruel and unnecessary. (Sure, if it's kill the cow or starve, then say your prayers, my bovine friend — but for now, it's not quite a mortal struggle to subsist on the other five food groups.) I am well-aware that even telling you this makes me seem like the kind of person who wants to break into your house and liberate your pet hamster — that is, like a PETA activist. Most vegetarians, though, would tell you that they appreciate the intentions of groups like PETA but not the obnoxious tactics. It's like this: We're all rooting for the same team, but they're the ones in face paint, bellowing obscenities at the umpire and flipping over every car with a Yankees bumper sticker. I have no designs on your Camry or your hamster.

Now, when I say that vegetarians are normal people with normal food cravings, many omnivores will hoist a lamb shank in triumph and point out that you can hardly call yourself normal if the aroma of, say, sizzling bacon doesn't fill you with deepest yearning. To which I reply: We're not 5 *insane*. We *know* meat tastes good; it's why there's a freezer case at your supermarket full of woefully inadequate meat substitutes. Believe me, if obtaining bacon didn't require slaughtering a pig, I'd have a BLT in each hand right now with a bacon layer cake waiting in the fridge for dessert. But, that said, I can also tell you that with some time away from the butcher's section, many meat products start to seem gross. Ground beef in particular now strikes me as absolutely revolting; I have a vague memory that hamburgers taste good, but the idea of taking a cow's leg, mulching it into a fatty pulp, and forming it into a pancake makes me gag. And hot dogs . . . I mean, *hot dogs*? You *do* know what that is, right?

As a consolation prize we get tofu, a treasure most omnivores are more than happy to do without. Well, this may stun you, but I'm not any more excited about a steaming heap of unseasoned tofu blobs than you are. Tofu is like fugu blowfish sushi: Prepared correctly, it's delicious; prepared incorrectly, it's lethal. Very early in my vegetarian career, I found myself famished and stuck in a mall, so I wandered over to the food court's Asian counter. When I asked the teenage chief culinary artisan what was in the tofu stir-fry, he snorted and replied, "Shit." Desperation made me order it anyway, and I can tell you that promises have rarely been more loyally kept than this guy's pledge that the tofu would taste like shit. So here's a tip: Unless you know you're in expert hands (Thai restaurants are a good bet), don't even try tofu. Otherwise, it's your funeral.

As long as we're discussing restaurants, allow me a quick word with the hardworking chefs at America's dining establishments. We really appreciate that you included a vegetarian option on your menu (and if you didn't, is our money not green?), but it may interest you to know that most of us are not salad freaks on a grim slog for nourishment. We actually enjoy food, especially the kind that tastes good. So enough with the bland vegetable dishes, and, for God's sake, *please* make the Garden-burgers stop; it's stunning how many restaurants lavish unending care on their meat dishes yet are content to throw a flavorless hockey puck from Costco into the microwave and call it cuisine. Every vegetarian is used to slim pickings when dining out, so we're not asking for much— just for something *you'd* like to eat. I'll even offer a handy trick. Pretend you're trapped in a kitchen stocked with every ingredient imaginable, from asiago to zucchini, but with zero meat. With no flesh available, picture what you'd make for yourself; this is what we want, too.

For those kind-hearted omnivores who willingly invite feral vegetarians into their homes for dinner parties and barbecues (really! we do that, too!), the same rule applies—but also know that unless you're dealing with an herbivore who is a prick for unrelated reasons, we don't expect you to bend over backward for us. In fact, if we get the sense that

you cooked for three extra hours to accommodate our dietary prefer-
ences, we will marvel at your considerate nature, but we will also feel
insanely guilty. Similarly, it's very thoughtful of you to ask whether it'll
bother me if I see you eat meat, but don't worry: I'm not going to com-
pose an epic poem about your club sandwich.

Which leads me to a vital point for friendly omnivore-herbivore rela-
tions. As you're enjoying that pork loin next to me, *I am not silently judg-
ing you.* I realize that anyone who has encountered the breed of smug
vegetarian who says things like, "I can hear your lunch screaming," will
find this tough to believe, but I'm honestly not out to convert you. My
girlfriend and my closest pals all eat meat, and they'll affirm that I've
never even raised an eyebrow about it. Now, do I think it strange that the
same people who dress their dogs in berets and send them to day spas
are often unfazed that an equally smart pig suffered and died to become
their McMuffin? Yes, I do. (Or, to use a more pressing example, how
many Americans will bemoan Eight Belles' fatal Kentucky Derby injury
tonight at the dinner table between bites of beef?) Would I prefer it if we
at least raised these animals humanely? Yes, I would.

Let's be honest, though: I'm not exactly St. Francis of Assisi over here,   10
tenderly ministering to every chipmunk that crosses my path. I try to
represent for the animal kingdom, but take a look at my shoes — they're
made of leather, which, I am told by those with expert knowledge of the
tanning process, comes from dead cows. This is the sort of revelation
that prompts meat boosters to pick up the triumphant lamb shank once
again and accuse us of hypocrisy. Well, *sort of.* (Hey, *you* try to find a pair
of nonleather dress shoes.) My dedication to the cause might be incom-
plete, but I'd still say that doing something beats doing nothing. It's kind
of like driving a hybrid: not a solution to the global-warming dilemma
but a decent start. Let's just say that at the dinner table, I roll in a Prius.

Finally, grant me one more cordial request: Please don't try to convince us that being vegetarian is somehow wrong. If you're concerned
for my health, that's very nice, though you can rest assured that I'm in
shipshape. If you want to have an amiable tête-à-tête about vegetarianism, that's great. But if you insist on being the aggressive blowhard who
takes meatlessness as a personal insult and rails about what fools we
all are, you're only going to persuade me that you're a dickhead. When
someone says he's Catholic, you probably don't start the stump speech
about how God is a lie created to enslave the ignorant masses, and it's
equally offensive to berate an herbivore. I know you think we're crazy.
That's neat. But seeing as I've endured the hassle of being a vegetarian
for several years now, perhaps I've given this a *little* thought. So let's just
agree to disagree and get on with making fun of Hillary Clinton's inability to operate a coffee machine.

4

Because, really, peace and understanding are what it's all about: your porterhouse and my portobello coexisting in perfect harmony—though preferably not touching. We're actually not so different, after all, my omnivorous chums. In fact, I like to think that when an omnivore looks in the mirror, he just sees a vegetarian who happens to eat meat. Or, no, wait, maybe the *mirror* sees the omnivore through the *prism* of flesh and realizes we all have a crystalline animal soul, you know?

This is excellent weed, by the way, if you want a hit. Hey, while you're here: Have I ever told you about hemp?

[2008]

NOEL PERRIN   [1927–2004]

The Androgynous Man

Noel Perrin was an educator and writer whose subjects included feu-
dal Japanese history, life in rural New England, and his adventures with
an electric car. He was educated at Williams College, Duke University,
and Cambridge University, England. For nearly forty years, Perrin
taught literature at Dartmouth College, where he was considered an
authority on the poetry of Robert Frost. Later in his career, Perrin
expanded his focus to include environmental studies, a choice made
after living for much of his life in a New England farmhouse. Perrin's
essays appeared in many publications, including *The Washington Post*.
In his "Rediscoveries" column, written monthly for many years, Perrin
examined writers whom he believed had been neglected and warranted
new attention. Perrin's essays depicting rural life were collected in several books, including *Vermont in All Weathers* (1973), *First Person Rural*
(1978), *Second Person Rural* (1980), and *Third Person Rural* (1982). In
"The Androgynous Man," which appeared in the *New York Times* in
1984, Perrin examines the restrictive nature of sexual stereotyping.

The summer I was 16, I took a train from New York to Steamboat Springs,
Colo., where I was going to be assistant wrangler at a camp. The trip took
three days, and since I was much too shy to talk to strangers, I had quite a
lot of time for reading. I read all of *Gone With the Wind*. I read all of the
interesting articles in a couple of magazines I had, and then I went back
and read all the dull stuff. I also took all the quizzes, a thing of which magazines were fuller then than now.

The one that held my undivided attention was called "How Masculine/
Feminine Are You?" It consisted of a large number of inkblots. The reader
was supposed to decide which of four objects each blot most resembled.
The choices might be a cloud, a steam-engine, a caterpillar and a sofa.

When I finished the test, I was shocked to find that I was barely masculine at all. On a scale of 1 to 10, I was about 1.2. Me, the horse wrangler?
(And not just wrangler, either. That summer, I had to skin a couple of
horses that died — the camp owner wanted the hides.)

6

The results of that test were so terrifying to me that for the first time in my life I did a piece of original analysis. Having unlimited time on the train, I looked at the "masculine" answers over and over, trying to find what it was that distinguished real men from people like me—and eventually I discovered two very simple patterns. It was "masculine" to think the blots looked like man-made objects, and "feminine" to think they looked like natural objects. It was masculine to think they looked like things capable of causing harm, and feminine to think of innocent things.

Even at 16, I had the sense to see that the compilers of the test were   5
using rather limited criteria—maleness and femaleness are both more complicated than that—and I breathed a hugh sigh of relief. I wasn't necessarily a wimp, after all.

That the test did reveal something other than the superficiality of its makers I realized only many years later. What it revealed was that there is a large class of men and women both, to which I belong, who are essentially androgynous. That doesn't mean we're gay, or low in the appropriate hormones, or uncomfortable performing the jobs traditionally assigned our sexes. (A few years after that summer, I was leading troops in combat and, unfashionable as it now is to admit this, having a very good time. War is exciting. What a pity the 20th century went and spoiled it with high-tech weapons.)

What it does mean to be spiritually androgynous is a kind of freedom. Men who are all-male, or he-man, or 100% red-blooded Americans, have a little biological set that causes them to be attracted to physical power, and probably also to dominance. Maybe even to watching football. I don't say this to criticize them. Completely masculine men are quite often wonderful people: good husbands, good (though sometimes overwhelming) fathers, good members of society. Furthermore, they are often so unself-consciously at ease in the world that other men seem to imitate them. They just aren't as free as androgynes. They pretty nearly have to be what they are; we have a range of choices open.

The sad part is that many of us never discover that. Men who are not 100% red-blooded Americans—say those who are only 75% red-blooded— often fail to notice their freedom. They are too busy trying to copy the he-men ever to realize that men, like women, come in a wide variety of acceptable types. Why this frantic imitation? My answer is mere speculation, but not casual. I have speculated on this for a long time.

Partly they're just envious of the he-man's unconscious ease. Mostly they're terrified of finding that there may be something wrong with them deep down, some weakness at the heart. To avoid discovering that, they spend their lives acting out the role that the he-man naturally lives. Sad.

One thing that men owe to the women's movement is that this kind of   10
failure is less common than it used to be. In releasing themselves from

the single ideal of the dependent woman, women have more or less incidentally released a lot of men from the single ideal of the dominant male. The one mistake the feminists have made, I think, is in supposing that all men need this release, or that the world would be a better place if all men achieved it. It wouldn't. It would just be duller.

So far I have been pretty vague about just what the freedom of the androgynous man is. Obviously it varies with the case. In the case I know best, my own, I can be quite specific. It has freed me most as a parent. I am, among other things, a fairly good natural mother. I like the nurturing role. It makes me feel good to see a child eat—and it turns me to mush to see a 4-year-old holding a glass with both small hands, in order to drink. I even enjoyed sewing patches on the knees of my daughter Amy's Dr. Dentons when she was at the crawling stage. All that pleasure I would have lost if I had made myself stick to the notion of the paternal role that I started with.

Or take a smaller and rather ridiculous example. I feel free to kiss cats. Until recently it never occurred to me that I would want to, though my daughters have been doing it all their lives. But my elder daughter is now 22, and in London. Of course, I get to look after her cat while she is gone. He's a big, handsome farm cat named Petrushka, very unsentimental though used from kittenhood to being kissed on the top of the head by Elizabeth. I've gotten very fond of him (he's the adventurous kind of cat who likes to climb hills with you), and one night I simply felt like kissing him on the top of the head, and did. Why did no one tell me sooner how silky cat fur is?

Then there's my relation to cars. I am completely unembarrassed by my inability to diagnose even minor problems in whatever object I happen to be driving, and don't have to make some insider's remark to mechanics to try to establish that I, too, am a "Man With His Machine."

The same ease extends to household maintenance. I do it, of course. Service people are expensive. But for the last decade my house has functioned better than it used to because I have had the aid of a volume called "Home Repairs Any Woman Can Do," which is pitched just right for people at my technical level. As a youth, I'd as soon have touched such a book as I would have become a transvestite. Even though common sense says there is really nothing sexual whatsoever about fixing sinks.

Or take public emotion. All my life I have easily been moved by certain 15 kinds of voices. The actress Siobhan McKenna's, to take a notable case. Give her an emotional scene in a play, and within ten words my eyes are full of tears. In boyhood, my great dread was that someone might notice. I struggled manfully, you might say, to suppress this weakness. Now, of course, I don't see it as a weakness at all, but as a kind of fulfillment. I even suspect that the true he-men feel the same way, or one kind of them does, at least, and it's only the poor imitators who have to struggle to repress themselves.

Let me come back to the inkblots, with their assumption that masculine equates with machinery and science, and feminine with art and nature. I have no idea whether the right pronoun for God is He, She, or It. But this I'm pretty sure of. If God could somehow be induced to take that test, God would not come out macho and not feminismo, either, but right in the middle. Fellow androgynes, it's a nice thought.

YVONNE LEDOUX

Through My Eyes

Yvonne LeDoux, a student at Pueblo Community College's Durango branch campus, is working towards an Associate of Arts degree. She is involved in a non-profit organization that helps with housing and enjoys community service. In the future she hopes to write for children.

Driving up to our new house seemed quite mysterious. I had a dejavu feeling in my gut. It was dark and hot; the smells were not the same. We were in Yemen. My father had taken a job with Tipton and Kalmbach, a company out of Denver. It was a water development project. I was fourteen, and the place was definitely out of the ordinary. We entered an encampment about a half a mile from the village. This was our new home. Our house was set up on stilts to keep the bugs out. The camp guard's home was set up by the front gates. The guard was from the village and had a daughter named Fatima; she was thirteen and had already been returned to him from a marriage. Next door lived Nageeb, Issam, and Majeeb from Cairo. I wanted to meet the children and learn the language. What I learned, to my amazement, was so much more and would be with me a lifetime. I learned about freedom: freedom to have choices, freedom to learn, and freedom to speak.

I took it for granted that in the United States we have freedom of choice. I never realized that children were leading such different lives elsewhere. I was a young girl myself. Fatima's choice for a husband had been that of her father. He had been given oxen and sheep in exchange for a bride. She was, I believe, nine years old when this occurred, and she was married to a man thirty years of age. Apparently, she was returned because she could not fulfill her duties, and thus she disgraced her family. Fatima was an outcast. Despite all she had been through, I loved her spirit and her smile. She was always happy to see us. She wanted to learn so much about us and our life, but she was discouraged, even punished, for doing so. It was her actions when her father was around that made us worry. We still managed to teach each other our languages, and we began to teach Fatima to write. I am sure there would have been dire repercussions for that if ever it had been found out. Education was definitely not a choice, especially for women. The village had no formal hut set aside for learning. There seemed to be no system.

Education was all based on religion and passed down through family. I thought, "What an obscure way to learn!" Girls were typically married off at a young age. They were somewhat discarded, treated less than men in value. It was not uncommon to see a man riding a camel with his wife following along on foot, carrying packages like a pack horse.

Women were often clothed from head to toe. The heat would lead one to believe that comfort should be a choice. It was not. It was their religious beliefs that set forth what would be appropriate clothing and what would not. If they were single, their faces were covered leaving only a slit for their eyes; married women, however, could show their faces. We often went to the beaches, but I cannot recall ever seeing a Yemeni woman swimming in the Red Sea. There was only the story of the lady from Britain. She was raped and then flogged because she was not wearing the appropriate clothing and had not screamed loudly enough.

In the United States we have freedom to speak. I never understood that so clearly as when I was visiting the neighbors in Yemen. Naggeb, Issam, and Majeed were eight, seven, and nine years old. Their mother spoke a little English. She often taught us songs and dances from her country. I thought it would be nice to tape her music and have her sing a few songs. I planned to share them with my school upon my return. Never had I witnessed such a strange event: a son slapping his mother hard on the face because her voice was not allowed to be taped or preserved for others to hear. Her son explained this to me angrily and requested that I leave his home. After a week we were allowed back, with restrictions. We were told that we were not to teach her our ways. They were of no benefit to her.

It was the men who had the authority. On one of our weekly excursions to the market, a young man, fifteen or so, was standing on the side of the road, his body covered with oozing lesions. This boy was begging for money. My father stopped and offered him what medicine we had with us in the first aid kit. The boy declined and accepted only the cash. While we were at the market, my father purchased ointment for the boy. On the return home, I was anxious but excited about helping this boy. We stopped. He was still there. It was sad because he appeared to be in so much pain and was very frail. My father reached out while I tried to explain to the boy about the medicine. All of a sudden, a man jumped out from behind the tall grasses and began to ward us off with a long stick. He was hitting my father. I jumped in the jeep. This was their means of survival... his son's suffering. His son had no voice of his own.

Freedom to speak out against what seemed to be atrocities was nonexistent in Yemen. The Yemenis settled for this life because it was all they knew. Traveling to Sana'a, the capital of Yemen, was a

11

weekend excursion for my family. It was nestled in the mountains, and we resided in the desert. So vivid is the memory for my sister and me. I think I can still feel the stares, the rage, and hatred these people had. My sister took off running into a crowd of people who were yelling and surrounding something. I noticed her standing there like time had stopped, and she was all I saw for an instant. It seemed like an hour. Her gaze was fixated on such a horrific sight; tears were streaming from her face. It was someone being stoned. The crowd was so thick we could hear only the wailing, the screaming cries. I covered her eyes. We tried to make our way through the crowd. It seemed like people were everywhere. They handed us stones to throw, and I have never seen such a glare as theirs-- eyes so hardened and piercing. This incident still haunts me to think of that day. My sister had trouble sleeping and did not want to travel to the city anymore. I just remember their eyes: brown with flecks of gold, rimmed with black, the whites so very white. The pupils were so intense and eerie. If that was the image of their souls, I tremble and cry for their hatred.

I learned a lot about freedom and dreams in Yemen. I realized that I had the possibility to become someone else. I could strive to make changes in my life. I understand not taking one's freedom for granted. We have the ability to speak and educate our minds and to accomplish the goals we establish in our lives with the choices we make. Freedom, sometimes, is taken so lightly. It is a great gift we should all cherish, especially since there are others who are not so fortunate.

DUSTIN WERTZ

Life on the Road

Dustin Wertz, a student at Pueblo Community College, is working on an Associate of Science Degree and hopes to work on environmental issues and travel the world. Dustin is an artist and an avid writer of short prose pieces.

As the sun is slowly disappearing across a vast sky and twilight begins to shade a landscape that is unfamiliar and unexplored, I begin to wonder where I will sleep tonight. Sleep is not hard to find when the days have been productive. The only time sleep on the road gets really rough is when the ground is wet or when it begins to get dark enough that finding a quiet place away from anyone who might blow my cover becomes paramount. Life on the road can be challenging if not a constant paradox between good and evil. Relying purely on instinct, the generosity of mankind, everything necessary for weeks strapped to a backpack, a proud thumb, a good pair of shoes, and enough gumption to stand for hours on the corner of some strange intersecting highways gesturing for a ride can, despite popular belief, be one of the most liberating experiences in the modern world.

I was gone for only three months, but in those three months I felt heart. I felt the beating, pulsating sensation that lies placidly beneath everything--beneath our surroundings, beneath people and animals, beneath the stars in the sky. But, mainly, I felt that in myself. I could actually feel that force breathing through me and coursing through my veins. And I could see it in the faces of people I would meet along the way, even in the faces of those elderly couples shopping in their neighborhood grocery store, wondering where this traveling hippie kid came from and what I was doing in their quiet little town. Even though their looks seemed to be criticizing, I could still sense the feeling of life and wonderment.

There are so many people out there, and the hitchhiker is bound to meet all different types of them while traveling: everyone from the revolutionaries, the protestors, the druggies, the homeless, the rich, the hungry whom I shared the last of my food with, the strict religious family who gave me a home to sleep in and didn't happen to say one word about their faith, the beautiful French girl who had no idea what I was saying, the crack head on the subway trying to cut my pants with a razor blade and steal my wallet, the typical old man pervert driving the van with no windows, the guy who couldn't stop talking about the chemical makeup of LSD, the doctor who let me stay with him in his chalet as he fed me three times a day then later paid me for small tasks I had helped him with, the lonely and the criticizing, and the weak to the strongest of minds. Overall, the people I met on the road were genuine and good natured, some more than others naturally. I miss my time on the road, and I honestly don't know what brought me back to the same exit I started from at the end of the same old town I grew up in.

The more I started to travel, the more tips and tricks I started to pick up on, things that I thought wouldn't even matter or even gave a second thought to before. For instance, when looking for a ride, I started to put my bag right in front of me, and I would always be standing when gesturing for a ride. I found the reason for this technique was that anyone who would ever consider me for a ride might not have the room, and my demeanor looked bad if I was just sitting there hoping someone would eventually stop. I found I had to present myself, have fun, smile, wave, be comical, and wear a silly hat. When drivers picked me up, I would talk to them as though I had known them for years, trying never to fall asleep even if I was extremely tired. I learned not to try to go hitchhiking at night; the best time to get a ride is early in the morning, shortly after the sun begins to rise. Another important simple truth is never to be afraid to turn someone down for a ride. If the driver wasn't going in the direction I had in mind, then I didn't take the ride. If I was going to a specific place, I would ask a lot of different people. This usually helped me navigate through bigger cities. This way I wouldn't feel as if I were running in circles all hours of the day. Also having room for things along the way is greatly beneficial. I would have never known I would complete the latter half of my trip with a bear scull in my bag, along with some other random possessions. I also found it very handy when food or water was given to me. I was taught and shown that if times get tough enough, everything the hitchhiker really needs to live can be taken from a dumpster. Sure, it's not the most pleasant topic to think about, but when I see someone happy because someone threw away a pair of brand new shoes or a warm jacket, it's not so bad.

In addition, my whole perspective on interacting with people shifted from the norm. I began to interpret things differently. I began to respect omens I may have once overlooked completely. I also began to interpret and analyze character much more in-depth. One of the only things that really upset me with people was when they would automatically assume that I was expecting a handout or that I was unkempt hygienically. These two things were the worst. I can still remember some of those people and their attitude towards me, how it actually made me sad that I couldn't get through to some of the people, even to say "hello," or "God bless you" when they sneezed. Some couldn't even look me in the eyes and purposefully chose to walk the long way around just so they didn't even have to pass me in crossing. I was never mean or hateful to anyone unless I felt physically threatened or was put into a compromising situation. I often thought that there should be more traveling kids out there to break the stereotypical mold of a transient junky asking for change.

As crazy as it may sound, I thought it would be a marvelous way for a child to spend his or her preschool days, not alone, of course, but with the appropriate parent, and only in the summer when the nights were warm enough to sleep outside. Some have called me crazy to even fathom the idea, but in my mind the life lessons and experience alone totally outweigh the normal methods of instilling values and morals into a young human being. I feel as if I had gone through that type of experience at such a young age, I would be more prepared and knowledgeable about the actual realities of life: how two different sides have two completely different angles and ways to interpret each. Also, if people want to jump and laugh and be free, then nothing should stop them; mundane life gives birth to simple beauty, and peace can most easily be found in chaos; death is just rebirth, and our time here is to be spent loving. It is no simpler than this: to love and be loved in return, to love nature and respect those uncontrollable forces. Respecting those feelings of the unexplained and mysterious, I have learned to face the unknown with open arms and to look into the darkness with open eyes and not be afraid of what I may find out. Good or bad, it is all part of a beautiful picture we as a whole have created and live within. And to gain a small grasp on how gorgeous everything really is underneath the veil is absolutely incomparable.

JULIE MAGBY

A Quiet Impact

Julie Magby returned to school at age 43 after raising her two children. Her major at Pueblo Community College is library technician with the long term goal of a master's degree in library and information science.

A petty criminal is sentenced to fifty hours of community service, Mother Theresa visits orphans, and a small town serves Thanksgiving dinner to the homeless. These are the types of volunteer activities that are reported in the news. However, volunteering goes much further than these highly publicized activities. It is the foundation of many communities, and it benefits the volunteer as well as the community that is being served. Whether looked at as an altruistic pursuit, a required duty, or an exploratory hobby, volunteering brings unexpected positive rewards.

Volunteering enriches the life of an individual. For example, community service for a criminal is not a punishment. Rather, it is an introduction to a positive interaction with society and possibly the first time the person has been shown a way to make a valuable contribution to his or her community; this interaction can lead to a healthy pride and the desire to be a better person. The altruistic idea of volunteering helps an individual see things from others' perspectives. From the very young to the very old, the variety of people met while volunteering is endless. Volunteer opportunities working directly with people can include working with disabled children, homeless individuals and families, and nursing homes and hospital patients. In sparsely populated areas, firefighters and EMTs are volunteers. By spending even a short time assisting in any of these areas, a volunteer meets a bouquet of characters, some pleasant and others thorny. The result is a deeper understanding and appreciation of human nature and our commonality.

Exploring new fields and sharing or learning new skills are other benefits of volunteering. Building projects such as Habitat for Humanity rely on skilled and unskilled volunteer construction workers, parents share sports skills while coaching city parks and recreation teams, and WWOOFies (Willing Workers on Organic Farms) learn organic gardening skills by volunteering to work for small farms. Office and leadership skills can be learned and practiced by volunteering at a variety of organizations. For example, when my sons were young, we "adopted-a-shelf" at our public library. This project not only gave them insight into some real life experience, such as filling out a time sheet, but also gave them references and experience to put on a job application when looking for their first paid jobs. Something unexpected was the fact that I discovered an interest in library work and have since made that my profession. Indeed, a few hours of volunteer time widens a person's outlook on the world while at the same time reliance on volunteers is essential for most communities.

If not for dedicated volunteers, many community services would have to be scaled back, if not completely eliminated. Many institutions have more volunteer employees than paid workers. For instance, a fire station where my husband volunteered had only a paid chief and a paramedic, who also worked for the neighboring districts. If there was a medical emergency, fire, or car wreck, the first responders, firemen, and EMTs were all trained volunteers. The fire station would have had to shut down if it hadn't been able to maintain enough volunteers, leaving the citizens in the hands of more distant neighboring districts. Animal rescues are also primarily kept running by volunteers. While working with my youngest son at the Humane Society, I noticed that everyone we interacted with, including our immediate supervisor, was an unpaid worker. These volunteers allowed for more animals to be cared for and a higher level of care than if only a few paid workers were doing the work. This unpaid workforce helps a city run more smoothly and accomplish more. Food banks, soup kitchens, emergency organizations, police departments, schools, national, state and city parks, hospitals, nursing homes, animal shelters, libraries, and museums make up the heart of any community, and they all rely on citizens to donate time.

Although most volunteers do not end up in a news story, they achieve a personal fulfillment while benefiting the community as a whole. They have the satisfaction of knowing they have offered help where it is needed. Moreover, they may have learned new skills or found a new career path. Facilitating a wide variety of tasks in an area, whether urban or rural, the volunteer quietly makes a monumental impact on his or her community.

JARED BROWN

CROSSing My Fingers and Hoping for FITness

Jared Brown competed in public speaking competitions at the national level in high school. After attending PCC, he plans to transfer to Colorado State University Pueblo to earn a BSN degree in nursing. Eventually, he hopes to complete a graduate nursing degree.

Sweat builds on my brow, lungs burn, muscles twitch with exhaustion, yet my shaking hands clench in anticipation to confront my sworn enemy. This enemy is the antagonist of all my fellow "skinny" kids: a weighted barbell, which wants nothing more than to embarrass us by clinging to the comfortable earth. There was a time when I would wish the workout for today included running, squats, or any other body-weight exercise, less taxing on my light frame. There was a time when this situation would be far from my mind, when I *knew* that I was too scrawny to challenge myself with heavily weighted workouts, and this daunting bar, holding one and a half times my bodyweight, was far from being thrown above my head. However, that was the time before I was introduced to CrossFit: the conditioning regimen that breaks barriers, builds confidence, changes lifestyle expectation, taking this skinny kid from the individual who would be carried away by a strong wind to one who is only a few small steps shy of Arnold Schwarzenegger!

Perhaps anyone who has seen me would say this is a slight exaggeration or even a flat-out lie, but I like to think that it merely shows the first strength increased by CrossFit—confidence. It is an internal strength with two major benefits: it can deafen the ears to those judgmental critiques, offering constant reminders of visible limitations, or, better yet, it can allow those disparagements to be heard more keenly! One benefit allows the confident individual to continue living the way he or she desires, while the other encourages that person to change for the better. If we are reminded of our flaws, confidence will help us create better goals and allow us to overcome them. This confidence first came into play in my life at a routine physical check-up. While I was sitting uncomfortably on the paper table-cover in the small, sterile room, my physician, with his eyes fixed on his clipboard, told me, "Jared, you appear to be a little too thin." An acute observation such as this begs the question whether this man's true vocation was to be a doctor or a detective. However, the only thought in my mind was to wonder why I was sitting in this office when I had mirrors at home which could give the same consultation for free. Yet with confidence, this was the moment when I truly heard the honest criticism and decided that this was something I could change. Now the more judgments people make about me, the more I feel challenged to improve and the more *confidence* empowers me to do so.

The second strength, which has been possessed by all of the most influential and inspiring figures in our lives, as well as every person who has achieved greatness, can be experienced as well in the CrossFit program—the strength to fail. Those who have feared to experience this feeling have never truly challenged themselves and will never be able to demonstrate their true potential. When I say CrossFit gives the strength to fail, I am not simply referring to being an expert at releasing a heavy barbell if the weight is more than I bargained for. The true strength that is found in failure is the knowledge it gives of personal limitations and the determination to overcome them. To press a substantial weight above my head to the point that I can no longer move it or do push-ups until my arms give out was downright uncomfortable at first, but soon it became the most satisfying feeling of accomplishment. I simply did not announce that this limit came after four pushups.

The last of these important inner strengths increased by CrossFit is one which extends far beyond a mere exercise regimen and can be seen in many aspects of life. It is perseverance. This is the strength that gives a CrossFit enthusiast the drive to continue, whether it is a hard workout with seemingly excessive cardio endurance or an even harder exercise with those sinister weighted bars. It can be seen in the businessperson working overtime to finish a project, the struggling student finishing the final paper late at night, or the gangly youngster who continues the marathon toward the next tempting mirage on the hot and dusty road, ignoring the birds circling above his head. Without perseverance, confidence is nothing more than a charade, and failure serves only to demoralize. When focused on an achievable goal, the correct motivation, and the help of a good breakfast, anyone can persevere and accomplish greatness.

It is better to explain CrossFit, not by describing how it offers a healthy lifestyle or a perfect beach-body, but by showcasing the conditioning it provides for a person's character, since it does not build just physical brawn but internal strength. CrossFit forces everyone out of his or her complacent comfort zone, driving the hulking weightlifter to run long distances and the spindly lightweight, only hoping to one day achieve fitness, to lift the heaviest weight he or she can. It is not the practically nonexistent muscle mass of my arm that will pull this barbell from the earth but the knowledge of my previous limits and the confidence to persevere beyond them. Those, my fellow "tooth picks," are the same powers that will change *your* life as well.

DAMIAN BORDENAVE

The Life and Times of a "Military Brat"

After living all over the world, **Damian Bordenave** moved with his family to Pueblo where he graduated from high school. He has been accepted at the Air Force Academy in Colorado Springs and will begin his training and education there in the fall of 2013.

When I was six years old, I remember going to my brothers' baseball game. We were living in Alamogordo, New Mexico, at the time because Holloman Air Force Base (AFB) was ten minutes down the road. At this particular baseball game, something happened that had never happened before to me. A gentleman at the concession stand stopped, looked at me for about ten seconds, and then finally said with a very perplexed look on his face, "What are you?" I thought about it for a while, and then I figured it out. Even though I didn't understand the question in the context in which he asked it, I came up with the answer that told him exactly what I was and how I identified myself at six years old. I told the gentleman "I'm military!"

Now even though I was not in fact "in the military," my father was a Lieutenant Colonel in the United States Air Force and retired after twenty-seven years of service. I was born in Pirmasens, Germany; lived in Wichita Falls, Texas; moved to Alamogordo, New Mexico; experienced life in Keflavik, Iceland; attended middle school in Del Rio, Texas; and finally "settled down" in Pueblo, Colorado. Indeed, I am a part of a unique and elite subculture of individuals who have a common bond unlike any other subculture in the world. Many who are members of this culture have gone on to be famous and influential people including Bill Cosby, Shaquille O'Neal, George Patton, John F. Kennedy, Mia Hamm, and numerous more businessmen and women, politicians, and athletes. I am, of course, referring to the culture that is the military brat. A military brat is, of course, the son or daughter of military personnel, but that biological definition hardly tells the whole story.

One of the many differences that distinguish a military brat from any other child in America is the response people get when they ask us either where we are from or where our hometown is. If a person were to ask a child from Pueblo where he was from, he would say Pueblo, but if a person asks a military brat, we typically answer in the following ways: "I'm a military brat. I'm from all over. Do you mean where did I live last? Do you mean where was I born or where do I live now?" We quickly learn the difference between a house and a home. A house is where we live, but our home is wherever the military sends us next.

Another difference between any other kid in America and a military brat is where our friends live. Most people's friends live in the city they live in. However, a military brat has friends in almost every state and in almost every country where there is a military post. Some friends with whom I still keep in touch live in Norway, Belgium, Germany, Italy, California, New York, Mississippi, New Mexico, Missouri, South Dakota, and Texas to name a few. When a military brat moves, we typically find friends whom we've either been stationed with before or find someone who happens to know a friend of ours whom we were stationed with before. For example, when I moved to Texas the second time, there was a family who was best friends with my cousins (who are also military brats) whom we met at church after we introduced ourselves as the Bordenaves. After about a year and a half of living in Texas, a person I went to school with in first grade in Iceland had moved to Texas, so we picked up where we had left off as if nothing had happened.

Military brats are respectful because our parents drilled respect into us. Our parents work for an organization which instills the values of duty, respect, honor, integrity, and other such qualities into them. As our parents are instilled with these values, they raise their family to adopt such values. We are brought up saying "yes, sir" and "no, sir" not because of their military meaning but simply because it's respectful. As such, we are brought up not talking back, not getting in fights, helping others, and other qualities which very much parallel the military but are in fact social niceties that are adhered to in polite company.

We are adaptable because we must be. Every new place we move to is unique and requires an amount of flexibility to fit in. There are cliques that have been established since pre-school that a military brat must work his or her way through to have friends. There are customs that the new place holds dear that a military brat must adopt. There may even be a hierarchy of some sort that military brats must be able to identify to ensure their next two to four years are enjoyable. Every move presents itself with a new list of challenges that through practice military brats have come to handle. Because of this practice, military brats are so adaptable.

It's hard to say why military brats are outgoing and leadership oriented, but this may go back to the parents too. We are taught to always do our best, so we become quite competitive. We have the opportunity to see our parents and the military in action, and there are not many better leader-oriented individuals or organizations in the world. We learn by our parents' example good leadership and a work ethic and model their behavior in whatever we do.

On the other hand, there are definitely misconceptions and hardships that we experience. One such misconception is the fact that we are called " brats." I have no idea where this term came from! All I know is that it's been around since longer than I've been alive. However, we are by no means "brats" in the sense that we are snobby, spoiled, or conceited.

A hardship that military brats must endure is not knowing what it is like growing up in one place. Many people who grow up in one place enjoy luxuries that military brats do not. Military brats miss out on growing up with the same friends for eighteen years. I have never had a face-to-face friend longer than about three years. Military brats miss out on having a place to call home. There's no one place I can return to and pick up where I left off or have people who are waiting for me.

One more hardship is how accustomed we become to saying good-bye. For instance, my senior year in high school, I found it hard to relate to people who were crying when they were saying their good-byes to friends they grew up with. As a military brat, it is not a question of if we'll be saying good-bye but when. Sometimes it's four years, and sometimes it's only two. But when the day comes and when Dad or Mom comes home and says he or she has orders, we ask where and when, then say our good-byes, and mend any broken fences before we go.

Military brats are a rare and distinctive breed. It's a blessing to experience cultures all over the world, meet unique individuals, and have the qualities of a well-rounded person. It's a curse when it comes time to say good-bye and work to fit in wherever we live next. But I consider it to have been a great privilege and experience that I wouldn't trade for the world and a badge of honor for anyone who says to someone "I'm military!"

JUDITH ORTIZ COFER   [b. 1952]

The Myth of the Latin Woman: I Just Met a Girl Named Maria

Judith Ortiz Cofer was born in Puerto Rico in 1952 and grew up there and in New Jersey. She is a poet, fiction writer, and autobiographer, and teaches literature and writing at the University of Georgia. Much of her work, such as her novel *The Line of the Sun* (1989) and *The Latin Deli: Prose and Poetry* (1993), explores her experiences as a Puerto Rican émigré and a Latina. Her most recent book is *Woman in Front of the Sun: Becoming a Writer* (2000).

"The Myth of the Latin Woman: I Just Met a Girl Named Maria" considers the stereotypes Americans hold about Latinas, and it does so through narrative and reflection. At the end of one of the stories she tells in her essay, dealing with an offensive man, Cofer writes, "My friend complimented me on my cool handling of the situation" (par. 10), then notes that what she really wanted to do was push the man into the pool. Notice, as you read, the ways in which Cofer is able in this essay, as in that incident, to strike a balance between anger and analysis.

On a bus trip to London from Oxford University where I was earning some graduate credits one summer, a young man, obviously fresh from a pub, spotted me and as if struck by inspiration went down on his knees in the aisle. With both hands over his heart he broke into an Irish tenor's rendition of "María" from *West Side Story*. My politely amused fellow passengers gave his lovely voice the round of gentle applause it deserved. Though I was not quite as amused, I managed my version of an English smile: no show of teeth, no extreme contortions of the facial muscles — I was at this time of my life practicing reserve and cool. Oh, that British control, how I coveted it. But María had followed me to London, reminding me of a prime fact of my life: you can leave the Island, master the English language, and travel as far as you can, but if you are a Latina, especially one like me who so obviously belongs to Rita Moreno's gene pool, the Island travels with you.

This is sometimes a very good thing—it may win you that extra minute of someone's attention. But with some people, the same things can make *you* an island—not so much a tropical paradise as an Alcatraz, a place nobody wants to visit. As a Puerto Rican girl growing up in the United States and wanting like most children to "belong," I resented the stereotype that my Hispanic appearance called forth from many people I met.

Our family lived in a large urban center in New Jersey during the sixties, where life was designed as a microcosm of my parents' casas on the island. We spoke in Spanish, we ate Puerto Rican food bought at the bodega, and we practiced strict Catholicism complete with Saturday confession and Sunday mass at a church where our parents were accommodated into a one-hour Spanish mass slot, performed by a Chinese priest trained as a missionary for Latin America.

As a girl I was kept under strict surveillance, since virtue and modesty were, by cultural equation, the same as family honor. As a teenager I was instructed on how to behave as a proper señorita. But it was a conflicting message girls got, since the Puerto Rican mothers also encouraged their daughters to look and act like women and to dress in clothes our Anglo friends and their mothers found too "mature" for our age. It was, and is, cultural, yet I often felt humiliated when I appeared at an American friend's party wearing a dress more suitable to a semiformal than to a playroom birthday celebration. At Puerto Rican festivities, neither the music nor the colors we wore could be too loud. I still experience a vague sense of letdown when I'm invited to a "party" and it turns out to be a marathon conversation in hushed tones rather than a fiesta with salsa, laughter, and dancing—the kind of celebration I remember from my childhood.

I remember Career Day in our high school, when teachers told us to come dressed as if for a job interview. It quickly became obvious that to the barrio girls, "dressing up" sometimes meant wearing ornate jewelry and clothing that would be more appropriate (by mainstream standards) for the company Christmas party than as daily office attire. That morning I had agonized in front of my closet, trying to figure out what a "career girl" would wear because, essentially, except for Marlo Thomas on TV, I had no models on which to base my decision. I knew how to dress for school: at the Catholic school I attended we all wore uniforms; I knew how to dress for Sunday mass, and I knew what dresses to wear for parties at my relatives' homes. Though I do not recall the precise details of my Career Day outfit, it must have been a composite of the above choices. But I remember a comment my friend (an Italian-American) made in later years that coalesced my impressions of that day. She said that at the business school she was attending the Puerto Rican girls al-

5

ways stood out for wearing "everything at once." She meant, of course, too much jewelry, too many accessories. On that day at school, we were simply made the negative models by the nuns who were themselves not credible fashion experts to any of us. But it was painfully obvious to me that to the others, in their tailored skirts and silk blouses, we must have seemed "hopeless" and "vulgar." Though I now know that most adolescents feel out of step much of the time, I also know that for the Puerto Rican girls of my generation that sense was intensified. The way our teachers and classmates looked at us that day in school was just a taste of the culture clash that awaited us in the real world, where prospective employers and men on the street would often misinterpret our tight skirts and jingling bracelets as a come-on.

Mixed cultural signals have perpetuated certain stereotypes—for example, that of the Hispanic woman as the "Hot Tamale" or sexual firebrand. It is a one-dimensional view that the media have found easy to promote. In their special vocabulary, advertisers have designated "sizzling" and "smoldering" as the adjectives of choice for describing not only the foods but also the women of Latin America. From conversations in my house I recall hearing about the harassment that Puerto Rican women endured in factories where the "boss men" talked to them as if sexual innuendo was all they understood and, worse, often gave them the choice of submitting to advances or being fired.

It is custom, however, not chromosomes, that leads us to choose scarlet over pale pink. As young girls, we were influenced in our decisions about clothes and colors by the women—older sisters and mothers who had grown up on a tropical island where the natural environment was a riot of primary colors, where showing your skin was one way to keep cool as well as to look sexy. Most important of all, on the island, women perhaps felt freer to dress and move more provocatively, since, in most cases, they were protected by the traditions, mores, and laws of a Spanish/Catholic system of morality and machismo whose main rule was: *You may look at my sister, but if you touch her I will kill you.* The extended family and church structure could provide a young woman with a circle of safety in her small pueblo on the island; if a man "wronged" a girl, everyone would close in to save her family honor.

This is what I have gleaned from my discussions as an adult with older Puerto Rican women. They have told me about dressing in their best party clothes on Saturday nights and going to the town's plaza to promenade with their girlfriends in front of the boys they liked. The males were thus given an opportunity to admire the women and to express their admiration in the form of *piropos*: erotically charged street poems they composed on the spot. I have been subjected to a few piropos while visiting the Island, and they can be outrageous, although custom dictates that they must never cross into obscenity. This ritual, as I understand it, also entails a show of studied indifference on the woman's part; if she is "decent," she must not acknowledge the man's impassioned words. So I do understand how things can be lost in translation. When a Puerto Rican girl dressed in her idea of what is attractive meets a man from the mainstream culture who has been trained to react to certain types of clothing as a sexual signal, a clash is likely to take place. The line I first heard based on this aspect of the myth happened when the boy who took me to my first formal dance leaned over to plant a sloppy overeager kiss painfully on my mouth, and when I didn't respond with sufficient passion said in a resentful tone: "I thought you Latin girls were supposed to mature early"—my first instance of being thought of as a fruit or vegetable—I was supposed to *ripen*, not just grow into womanhood like other girls.

It is surprising to some of my professional friends that some people, including those who should know better, still put others "in their place." Though rarer, these incidents are still commonplace in my life. It happened to me most recently during a stay at a very classy metropolitan hotel favored by young professional couples for their weddings. Late one evening after the theater, as I walked toward my room with my new colleague (a woman with whom I was coordinating an arts program), a middle-aged man in a tuxedo, a young girl in satin and lace on his arm, stepped directly into our path. With his champagne glass extended toward me, he exclaimed, "Evita!"

Our way blocked, my companion and I listened as the man half-recited, half-bellowed "Don't Cry for Me, Argentina." When he finished, the young girl said: "How about a round of applause for my daddy?" We complied, hoping this would bring the silly spectacle to a close. I was becoming aware that our little group was attracting the attention of the other guests. "Daddy" must have perceived this too, and he once more barred the way as we tried to walk past him. He began to shout-sing a ditty to the tune of "La Bamba"—except the lyrics were about a girl named María whose exploits all rhymed with her name and gonorrhea. The girl kept saying "Oh, Daddy" and looking at me with pleading eyes. She wanted me to laugh along with the others. My companion and I stood silently waiting for the man to end his offensive song. When he finished, I looked not at him but at his daughter. I advised her calmly never to ask her father what he had done in the army. Then I walked between them and to my room. My friend complimented me on my cool handling of the situation. I confessed to her that I really had wanted to push the jerk into the swimming pool. I knew that this same man—probably a corporate executive, well educated, even worldly by most standards—would not have been likely to regale a white woman with a dirty song in

10

public. He would perhaps have checked his impulse by assuming that she could be somebody's wife or mother, or at least *somebody* who might take offense. But to him, I was just an Evita or a María: merely a character in his cartoon-populated universe.

Because of my education and my proficiency with the English language, I have acquired many mechanisms for dealing with the anger I experience. This was not true for my parents, nor is it true for the many Latin women working at menial jobs who must put up with stereotypes about our ethnic group such as: "They make good domestics." This is another facet of the myth of the Latin woman in the United States. Its origin is simple to deduce. Work as domestics, waitressing, and factory jobs are all that's available to women with little English and few skills. The myth of the Hispanic menial has been sustained by the same media phenomenon that made "Mammy" from *Gone with the Wind* America's idea of the black woman for generations: María, the housemaid or counter girl, is now indelibly etched into the national psyche. The big and the little screens have presented us with the picture of the funny Hispanic maid, mispronouncing words and cooking up a spicy storm in a shiny California kitchen.

This media-engendered image of the Latina in the United States has been documented by feminist Hispanic scholars, who claim that such portrayals are partially responsible for the denial of opportunities for upward mobility among Latinas in the professions. I have a Chicana friend working on a Ph.D. in philosophy at a major university. She says her doctor still shakes his head in puzzled amazement at all the "big words" she uses. Since I do not wear my diplomas around my neck for all to see, I too have on occasion been sent to that "kitchen," where some think I obviously belong.

One such incident that has stayed with me, though I recognize it as a minor offense, happened on the day of my first public poetry reading. It took place in Miami in a boat-restaurant where we were having lunch before the event. I was nervous and excited as I walked in with my notebook in my hand. An older woman motioned me to her table. Thinking (foolish me) that she wanted me to autograph a copy of my brand-new slender volume of verse, I went over. She ordered a cup of coffee from me, assuming that I was the waitress. Easy enough to mistake my poems for menus, I suppose. I know that it wasn't an intentional act of cruelty, yet of all the good things that happened that day, I remember that scene most clearly, because it reminded me of what I had to overcome before anyone would take me seriously. In retrospect I understand that my anger gave my reading fire, that I have almost always taken doubts in my abilities as a challenge—and that the result is, most times, a feeling of satisfaction at having won a convert when I see the cold, appraising eyes warm to my words, the body language change, the smile that indicates that I have opened some avenue for communication. That day I read to that woman and her lowered eyes told me that she was embarrassed at her little faux pas, and when I willed her to look up at me, it was my victory, and she graciously allowed me to punish her with my full attention. We shook hands at the end of the reading, and I never saw her again. She has probably forgotten the whole thing but maybe not.

Yet I am one of the lucky ones. My parents made it possible for me to acquire a stronger footing in the mainstream culture by giving me the chance at an education. And books and art have saved me from the harsher forms of ethnic and racial prejudice that many of my Hispanic *compañeras* have had to endure. I travel a lot around the United States, reading from my books of poetry and my novel, and the reception I most often receive is one of positive interest by people who want to know more about my culture. There are, however, thousands of Latinas without the privilege of an education or the entrée into society that I have. For them life is a struggle against the misconceptions perpetuated by the myth of the Latina as whore, domestic or criminal. We cannot change this by legislating the way people look at us. The transformation, as I see it, has to occur at a much more individual level. My personal goal in my public life is to try to replace the old pervasive stereotypes and myths about Latinas with a much more interesting set of realities. Every time I give a reading, I hope the stories I tell, the dreams and fears I examine in my work, can achieve some universal truth which will get my audience past the particulars of my skin color, my accent, or my clothes.

I once wrote a poem in which I called us Latinas "God's brown daugh- 15
ters." This poem is really a prayer of sorts, offered upward, but also, through the human-to-human channel of art, outward. It is a prayer for communication, and for respect. In it, Latin women pray "in Spanish to an Anglo God/with a Jewish heritage," and they are "fervently hoping/ that if not omnipotent,/at least He be bilingual."

[1992]

29

MALCOLM GLADWELL [b. 1963]

The Tipping Point

Born in England in 1963 to an English father and a West Indian
mother, **Malcolm Gladwell** immigrated with his parents to Canada as
a child. Gladwell received his bachelor's degree in history from the
University of Toronto, after which he began his writing career at the
American Spectator. He subsequently served with the *Washington Post*,
first as a business and science reporter and later as chief of the *Post's*
New York City bureau. While working as a staff writer for the *New
Yorker*, where he has spent more than fifteen years, Gladwell became
known for his highly readable articles that synthesize complex
research in the sciences and social sciences. He has won numerous
awards, including a National Magazine Award for his 1999 profile of
Ron Popeil, and in 2005, he was named among the top one hundred
most influential people in the world by *Time*. His books include *Blink:
The Power of Thinking without Thinking* (2005) and *Outliers: The Story
of Success* (2008). His latest work, *What the Dog Saw: And Other Adventures* (2009), is a compilation of his contributions to the *New Yorker*.

Gladwell's best-selling book *The Tipping Point: How Little Things Can
Make a Big Difference*, an examination of why change occurs, was published in 2000. The title of the book—and of this excerpt—comes
from epidemiology. As Gladwell defined it in an interview, the tipping
point is "the name given to that moment in an epidemic when a virus
reaches critical mass." Here, Gladwell focuses on the dramatic
decrease in New York City's violent crime rate during the 1990s. The
decrease, as he explains, was fueled in large part by strict policing of
more minor crimes.

During the 1990s violent crime declined across the United States for a
number of fairly straightforward reasons. The illegal trade in crack
cocaine, which had spawned a great deal of violence among gangs and
drug dealers, began to decline. The economy's dramatic recovery meant
that many people who might have been lured into crime got legitimate

jobs instead, and the general aging of the population meant that there were fewer people in the age range—males between eighteen and twenty-four—that is responsible for the majority of all violence. The question of why crime declined in New York City, however, is a little more complicated. In the period when the New York epidemic tipped down, the city's economy hadn't improved. It was still stagnant. In fact, the city's poorest neighborhoods had just been hit hard by the welfare cuts of the early 1990s. The waning of the crack cocaine epidemic in New York was clearly a factor, but then again, it had been in steady decline well before crime dipped. As for the aging of the population, because of heavy immigration to New York in the 1980s, the city was getting younger in the 1990s, not older. In any case, all of these trends are long-term changes that one would expect to have gradual effects. In New York the decline was anything but gradual. Something else clearly played a role in reversing New York's crime epidemic.

The most intriguing candidate for that "something else" is called the Broken Windows theory. Broken Windows was the brainchild of the criminologists James Q. Wilson and George Kelling. Wilson and Kelling argued that crime is the inevitable result of disorder. If a window is broken and left unrepaired, people walking by will conclude that no one cares and no one is in charge. Soon, more windows will be broken, and the sense of anarchy will spread from the building to the street on which it faces, sending a signal that anything goes. In a city, relatively minor problems like graffiti, public disorder, and aggressive panhandling, they write, are all the equivalent of broken windows, invitations to more serious crimes:

> Muggers and robbers, whether opportunistic or professional, believe they reduce their chances of being caught or even identified if they operate on streets where potential victims are already intimidated by prevailing conditions. If the neighborhood cannot keep a bothersome panhandler from annoying passersby, the thief may reason, it is even less likely to call the police to identify a potential mugger or to interfere if the mugging actually takes place.

This is an epidemic theory of crime. It says that crime is contagious— just as a fashion trend is contagious—that it can start with a broken window and spread to an entire community. The Tipping Point in this epidemic, though, isn't a particular kind of person—a Connector like Lois Weisberg or a Maven like Mark Alpert.[1] It's something physical like graffiti. The impetus to engage in a certain kind of behavior is not coming from a certain kind of person but from a feature of the environment.

In the mid-1980s Kelling was hired by the New York Transit Authority as a consultant, and he urged them to put the Broken Windows theory into practice. They obliged, bringing in a new subway director by the name of David Gunn to oversee a multibillion-dollar rebuilding of the subway system. Many subway advocates, at the time, told Gunn not to worry about graffiti, to focus on the larger questions of crime and subway reliability, and it seemed like reasonable advice. Worrying about graffiti at a time when the entire system was close to collapse seems as pointless as scrubbing the decks of the *Titanic* as it headed toward the icebergs. But Gunn insisted. "The graffiti was symbolic of the collapse of the system," he says. "When you looked at the process of rebuilding the organization and morale, you had to win the battle against graffiti. Without winning that battle, all the management reforms and physical changes just weren't going to happen. We were about to put out new trains that were worth about ten million bucks apiece, and unless we did something to protect them, we knew just what would happen. They would last one day and then they would be vandalized."

Gunn drew up a new management structure and a precise set of goals and timetables aimed at cleaning the system line by line, train by train. He started with the number seven train that connects Queens to midtown Manhattan, and began experimenting with new techniques to clean off the paint. On stainless-steel cars, solvents were used. On the painted cars, the graffiti were simply painted over. Gunn made it a rule that there should be no retreat, that once a car was "reclaimed" it should never be allowed to be vandalized again. "We were religious about it," Gunn said. At the end of the number one line in the Bronx, where the trains stop before turning around and going back to Manhattan, Gunn set up a cleaning station. If a car came in with graffiti, the graffiti had to be removed during the changeover, or the car was removed from service. "Dirty" cars, which hadn't yet been cleansed of graffiti, were never to be mixed with "clean" cars. The idea was to send an unambiguous message to the vandals themselves.

---

[1]In an earlier chapter of *The Tipping Point*, Gladwell discusses personality types who trigger major changes in society. Connectors have unusually large social circles, and Mavens are particularly knowledgeable about products, services, and prices. Lois Weisberg and Mark Alpert are two typical Americans whom Gladwell interviewed to illustrate these types.

"We had a yard up in Harlem on One hundred thirty-fifth Street where   5
the trains would lay up over night," Gunn said. "The kids would come
the first night and paint the side of the train white. Then they would
come the next night, after it was dry, and draw the outline. Then they
would come the third night and color it in. It was a three-day job. We
knew the kids would be working on one of the dirty trains, and what we
would do is wait for them to finish their mural. Then we'd walk over
with rollers and paint it over. The kids would be in tears, but we'd just be
going up and down, up and down. It was a message to them. If you want
to spend three nights of your time vandalizing a train, fine. But it's never
going to see the light of day."

Gunn's graffiti cleanup took from 1984 to 1990. At that point, the Transit Authority hired William Bratton to head the transit police, and the
second stage of the reclamation of the subway system began. Bratton
was, like Gunn, a disciple of Broken Windows. He describes Kelling, in
fact, as his intellectual mentor, and so his first step as police chief was as
seemingly quixotic as Gunn's. With felonies—serious crimes—on the
subway system at an all-time high, Bratton decided to crack down on
fare-beating. Why? Because he believed that, like graffiti, fare-beating
could be a signal, a small expression of disorder that invited much more
serious crimes. An estimated 170,000 people a day were entering the system, by one route or another, without paying a token. Some were kids,
who simply jumped over the turnstiles. Others would lean backward on
the turnstiles and force their way through. And once one or two or three
people began cheating the system, other people—who might never
otherwise have considered evading the law—would join in, reasoning
that if some people weren't going to pay, they shouldn't either, and the
problem would snowball. The problem was exacerbated by the fact fare-
beating was not easy to fight. Because there was only $1.25 at stake, the
transit police didn't feel it was worth their time to pursue it, particularly
when there were plenty of more serious crimes happening down on the
platform and in the trains.

Bratton is a colorful, charismatic man, a born leader, and he quickly
made his presence felt. His wife stayed behind in Boston, so he was free
to work long hours, and he would roam the city on the subway at night,
getting a sense of what the problems were and how best to fight them.
First, he picked stations where fare-beating was the biggest problem,
and put as many as ten policemen in plainclothes at the turnstiles. The
team would nab fare-beaters one by one, handcuff them, and leave them
standing, in a daisy chain, on the platform until they had a "full catch."
The idea was to signal, as publicly as possible, that the transit police
were now serious about cracking down on fare-beaters. Previously,
police officers had been wary of pursuing fare-beaters because the

arrest, the trip to the station house, the filling out of necessary forms, and the waiting for those forms to be processed took an entire day—all for a crime that usually merited no more than a slap on the wrist. Bratton retrofitted a city bus and turned it into a rolling station house, with its own fax machines, phones, holding pen, and fingerprinting facilities. Soon the turnaround time on an arrest was down to an hour. Bratton also insisted that a check be run on all those arrested. Sure enough, one out of seven arrestees had an outstanding warrant for a previous crime, and one out of twenty was carrying a weapon of some sort. Suddenly it wasn't hard to convince police officers that tackling fare-beating made sense. "For the cops it was a bonanza," Bratton writes. "Every arrest was like opening a box of Cracker Jack. What kind of toy am I going to get? Got a gun? Got a knife? Got a warrant? Do we have a murderer here? . . . After a while the bad guys wised up and began to leave their weapons home and pay their fares." Under Bratton, the number of ejections from subway stations—for drunkenness, or improper behavior—tripled within his first few months in office. Arrests for misdemeanors, for the kind of minor offenses that had gone unnoticed in the past, went up five-fold between 1990 and 1994. Bratton turned the transit police into an organization focused on the smallest infractions, on the details of life underground.

After the election of Rudolph Giuliani as mayor of New York in 1994, Bratton was appointed head of the New York City Police Department, and he applied the same strategies to the city at large. He instructed his officers to crack down on quality-of-life crimes: on the "squeegee men" who came up to drivers at New York City intersections and demanded money for washing car windows, for example, and on all the other above-ground equivalents of turnstile-jumping and graffiti. "Previous police administration had been handcuffed by restrictions," Bratton says. "We took the handcuffs off. We stepped up enforcement of the laws against public drunkenness and public urination and arrested repeat violators, including those who threw empty bottles on the street or were involved in even relatively minor damage to property. . . . If you peed in the street, you were going to jail." When crime began to fall in the city—as quickly and dramatically as it had in the subways—Bratton and Giuliani pointed to the same cause. Minor, seemingly insignificant quality-of-life crimes, they said, were Tipping Points for violent crime.

[2000]

AMITAI ETZIONI   [b. 1929]

Working at McDonald's

Born Werner Falk in 1929 in Cologne, Germany, **Amitai Etzioni** fled from Nazi Germany to Palestine in the 1930s, ultimately studying at the Hebrew University in Jerusalem. A prominent sociologist, he received his Ph.D. in 1958 from the University of California, Berkeley, and then taught for two decades at Columbia University. From 1979 to 1980 he served at the White House as a senior adviser on domestic affairs. The author of twenty-four books, including *The Monochrome Society* (2001), *The Limits of Privacy* (1999), and *The New Golden Rule* (1996), Etzioni has taught at George Washington University since 1980. As director of the university's Institute for Communitarian Policy Studies, Etzioni founded the Communitarian Network, a nonprofit, nonpartisan organization that provides a forum for discussing the impact of moral, social, and political issues on society's well being. He is also the founder of the journal *Responsive Community* and has been awarded numerous honors, including the 2001 John P. McGovern Award in Behavioral Sciences and the Seventh James Wilbur Award for Extraordinary Contributions to the Appreciation and Advancement of Human Values by the Conference on Value Inquiry.

Etzioni's "Working at McDonald's," originally published in the *Miami Herald* in 1986, evaluates the educational merits of adolescents' holding down part-time, paying jobs in fast-food restaurants. Critical of the long hours, the managerial role models, the failure of these jobs to foster independent thought and decision making skills, and the enticements of a questionable consumerism, Etzioni insists that teens "go back to school."

McDonald's is bad for your kids. I do not mean the flat patties and the white-flour buns; I refer to the jobs teen-agers undertake, mass-producing these choice items.

As many as two-thirds of America's high school juniors and seniors now hold down part-time paying jobs, according to studies. Many of these are in fast-food chains, of which McDonald's is the pioneer, trend-setter, and symbol.

Amitai Etzioni, "Working at McDonald's" from *The Miami Herald*, August 24, 1986. Reprinted by permission of the author.

At first, such jobs may seem right out of the Founding Fathers' educational manual for how to bring up self-reliant, work-ethic-driven, productive youngsters. But in fact, these jobs undermine school attendance and involvement, impart few skills that will be useful in later life, and simultaneously skew the values of teen-agers—especially their ideas about the worth of a dollar.

It has been a longstanding American tradition that youngsters ought to get paying jobs. In folklore, few pursuits are more deeply revered than the newspaper route and the sidewalk lemonade stand. Here the youngsters are to learn how sweet are the fruits of labor and self-discipline (papers are delivered early in the morning, rain or shine), and the ways of trade (if you price your lemonade too high or too low . . .).

Roy Rogers, Baskin Robbins, Kentucky Fried Chicken, *et al.*, may at   5
first seem nothing but a vast extension of the lemonade stand. They provide very large numbers of teen jobs, provide regular employment, pay quite well compared to many other teen jobs, and, in the modern equivalent of toiling over a hot stove, test one's stamina.

Closer examination, however, finds the McDonald's kind of job highly uneducational in several ways. Far from providing opportunities for entrepreneurship (the lemonade stand) or self- discipline, self-supervision, and self-scheduling (the paper route), most teen jobs these days are highly structured—what social scientists call "highly routinized."

True, you still have to have the gumption to get yourself over to the hamburger stand, but once you don the prescribed uniform, your task is spelled out in minute detail. The franchise prescribes the shape of the coffee cups; the weight, size, shape, and color of the patties; and the texture of the napkins (if any). Fresh coffee is to be made every eight minutes. And so on. There is no room for initiative, creativity, or even elementary rearrangements. These are breeding grounds for robots working for yesterday's assembly lines, not tomorrow's high-tech posts.

There are very few studies of the matter. One of the few is a 1984 study by Ivan Charper and Bryan Shore Fraser. The study relies mainly on what teen-agers write in response to questionnaires rather than actual observations of fast-food jobs. The authors argue that the employees develop many skills such as how to operate a food-preparation machine and a cash register. However, little attention is paid to how long it takes to acquire such a skill, or what its significance is.

What does it matter if you spend 20 minutes to learn to use a cash register, and then—"operate" it? What skill have you acquired? It is a long way from learning to work with a lathe or carpenter tools in the olden days or to program computers in the modern age.

A 1980 study by A. V. Harrell and P. W. Wirtz found that, among those   10
students who worked at least 25 hours per week while in school, their

unemployment rate four years later was half of that of seniors who did not work. This is an impressive statistic. It must be seen, though, together with the finding that many who begin as part-time employees in fast-food chains drop out of high school and are gobbled up in the world of low-skill jobs.

Some say that while these jobs are rather unsuited for college-bound, white, middle-class youngsters, they are "ideal" for lower-class, "non-academic," minority youngsters. Indeed, minorities are "over-represented" in these jobs (21 percent of fast-food employees). While it is true that these places provide income, work, and even some training to such youngsters, they also tend to perpetuate their disadvantaged status. They provide no career ladders, few marketable skills, and undermine school attendance and involvement.

The hours are often long. Among those 14 to 17, a third of fast-food employees (including some school dropouts) labor more than 30 hours per week, according to the Charper-Fraser study. Only 20 percent work 15 hours or less. The rest: between 15 to 30 hours.

Often the stores close late, and after closing one must clean up and tally up. In affluent Montgomery County, Md., where child labor would not seem to be a widespread economic necessity, 24 percent of the seniors at one high school in 1985 worked as much as five to seven days a week; 27 percent, three to five. There is just no way such amounts of work will not interfere with school work, especially homework. In an informal survey published in the most recent yearbook of the high school, 58 percent of the seniors acknowledged that their jobs interfere with their school work.

The Charper-Fraser study sees merit in learning teamwork and working under supervision. The authors have a point here. However, it must be noted that such learning is not automatically educational or whole-some. For example, much of the supervision in fast-food places leans toward teaching one the wrong kinds of compliance: blind obedience, or shared alienation with the "boss."

Supervision is often both tight and woefully inappropriate. Today, 15 fast-food chains and other such places of work (record shops, bowling alleys) keep costs down by having teens supervise teens with often no adult on the premises.

There is no father or mother figure with which to identify, to emulate, to provide a role model and guidance. The work-culture varies from one place to another: Sometimes it is a tightly run shop (must keep the cash registers ringing); sometimes a rather loose pot party interrupted by customers. However, only rarely is there a master to learn from, or much worth learning. Indeed, far from being places where solid adult work values are being transmitted, these are places where all too often delinquent teen values dominate. Typically, when my son Oren was dishing out ice cream for Baskin Robbins in upper Manhattan, his fellow teen-workers considered him a sucker for not helping himself to the till. Most youngsters felt they were entitled to $50 severance "pay" on their last day on the job.

The pay, oddly, is the part of the teen work-world that is most difficult to evaluate. The lemonade stand or paper route money was for your allowance. In the old days, apprentices learning a trade from a master contributed most, if not all of their income to their parents' household. Today, the teen pay may be low by adult standards, but it is often, especially in the middle class, spent largely or wholly by the teens. That is, the youngsters live free at home ("after all, they are high school kids") and are left with very substantial sums of money.

Where this money goes is not quite clear. Some use it to support themselves, especially among the poor. More middle-class kids set some money aside to help pay for college, or save it for a major purchase—often a car. But large amounts seem to flow to pay for an early introduction into the most trite aspects of American consumerism: Flimsy punk clothes, trinkets, and whatever else is the last fast-moving teen craze.

One may say that this is only fair and square; they are being good American consumers and spend their money on what turns them on. At least, a cynic might add, these funds do not go into illicit drugs and booze. On the other hand, an educator might bemoan that these young, yet unformed individuals, so early in life are driven to buy objects of no intrinsic educational, cultural, or social merit, learn so quickly the dubious merit of keeping up with the Joneses in ever-changing fads, promoted by mass merchandising.

Many teens find the instant reward of money, and the youth status 20 symbols it buys, much more alluring than credits in calculus courses, European history, or foreign languages. No wonder quite a few would rather skip school—and certainly homework—and instead work longer at a Burger King. Thus, most teen work these days is not providing early lessons in work ethic; it fosters escape from school and responsibilities, quick gratification, and a short cut to the consumeristic aspects of adult life.

Thus, parents should look at teen employment not as automatically educational. It is an activity—like sports—that can be turned into an educational opportunity. But it can also easily be abused. Youngsters must learn to balance the quest for income with the needs to keep growing and pursue other endeavors that do not pay off instantly—above all education.

Go back to school.

DUSTIN WERTZ

Tumbleweed Poetry Night

Dustin Wertz, a student at Pueblo Community College, is working on an Associate of Science Degree and hopes to work on environmental issues and travel the world. Dustin is an artist and an avid writer of short prose pieces.

Imagine sitting in a tiny coffee house, sipping an espresso, and listening to a mad man rant, as people snap their fingers to the beat of one crazy performance. Years ago, scenes like these were common. Anyone who was "in the know" was part of this subculture and contributed wholeheartedly to its success. Since then, many years have passed, cultures have changed, and what was once regarded as popular is now completely different. To find a scene like the one described above is almost as hard as trying to catch a falling star. If the coffee and the snapping audience are taken away, what is left is poetry night at the Tumbleweed Bookstore in Pueblo, Colorado, one of the only places in 2007 that offers a free poetry night that is always entertaining and thought-provoking.

The Tumbleweed Bookstore is a unique place to host a poetry night. One night every month, the doors open after hours to a secret society ambiance. As people begin to show up, they make their way to the large room toward the back. With a back-drop of classic, dusty old books, chairs begin to form a circle in the middle of the room. With lamplight as the only form of illumination, the crowd begins to unveil their latest installments, waiting patiently to share them with an unbiased crowd. Often times, it feels that a secret handshake might be required to gain entrance to the back room or that an old bookshelf had to be moved in order to find a stairway that leads to a basement conference room. But no such handshake or staircase exists.

Although poetry night may be designated for a specific crowd, the people who attend are always unhurried and easygoing. The platform for the readings is set up on an open forum, where everyone gets a chance to present his or her writings to a group of skilled and semi-professional writers. Most of the retired professionals who show up are published writers, still writing because they have a love and passion for literature. Many are weathered men who have deep stares and a certain countenance about them that can only be described as lives well lived. They smile with a genuine concern, never looking over their shoulders to see death slowly looming behind them. None of these men are waiting for the black chariot to fall from the heavens, for they are the true lovers of life; and not even death can take that away from them. However, not all who attend are so close to the touch of the reaper, although it can be felt that those who are closer to death have a large appreciation for life. The younger audiences who attend seem to have a special gaze about them. They have a sparkle in their eyes, a sparkle that many have once had, but lost when they stopped appreciating the simple things in life.

However, the actual poetry is the highlight of the evening. The majority of the poems are heartfelt works of love, disaster, pain, sorrow, happiness, wanderlust, greed, and desire. Many are written in the style of the Beat Generation authors, such as Kerouac and Ginsberg, as well as some excellent stream-of-consciousness writings that add to the overall feel of a generation not restricted by politics, religion, or stereotypes. The poetry represents a creative process almost lost in the dark slums of an untouched bookshelf or tucked away in the quiet, muffled rambling of people turned away for unpopular beliefs

We feel life through many different forms of expression. The poetry nights at the Tumbleweed Bookstore are one of the most undeniable signs that a love of life exists in Pueblo and that kind of heart hasn't been felt in years. Overall, the evenings spent at the Tumbleweed are well worth every minute. Even if just to get a taste, I highly recommend that any lover of literature sits in on a couple readings.

BRITTANY ALARID

Story Time at the Public Library

Brittany Alarid was part of the Early College Program at PCC and will graduate with an AA degree and an emphasis in elementary education. She plans to complete her B.A. at Colorado State University, Pueblo, and fulfill her dream of teaching young children.

Parents, imagine this. You are sitting in a quiet space in the public library, watching your child have the time of her life as she is being read to, book after book. You watch the intense gaze of her small, young face. She is learning and growing and having fun. All you have to do is sit back, relax, and enjoy the benefits of pre-school story time. It sounds great, doesn't it? It is, and it's just a jump, hop, and skip away. Pre-school story hour at the public library is an excellent program for young children because it's enjoyable, the stories are exciting, it's educational, and it enhances the parent/child relationship.

The most important achievement for pre-schoolers at story time is having fun. With the story-telling room resembling a home environment and making the children feel comfortable, it's hard not to! The over-stuffed chair, its adjacent floor lamp, and large area rug allow the children to relax and fully absorb the stories. The children's smiles and laughter as they sit next to their friends, old and new, tell of the fun soon to come. Their pleasure is unconcealed and contagious to everyone who enters the room. The visually pleasing books with distinct colors, shapes, textures, and designs that the story-teller selects add to the excitement of these young minds. The props, such as the peacock feather which accompanied the comical book *Where the Wild Things Are* by Maurice Sendak, are enjoyed by story-teller and children alike,   Furthermore, the stories themselves extend the children's fun. The stories that interest them keep their attention for the half hour story time. The characters, story, time, and setting of the selected books add to the excitement of what the children are listening to. Books are the best sources for children's education and development and become children's life-long friends. When these books are read with the story-teller's jubilant and delightful manner, children treasure these books and memories forever.

41

Also, this outstanding program is beneficial to the early development of pre-school children. Books are the basis of education especially for young children. When children are read to, they accumulate basic reading skills that last a lifetime and benefit them through their learning experiences. That's the sole reason for story hour: to help children become better readers. They learn reading comprehension, picture/story relationships, and basic vocabulary and spelling skills when they are read to and asked about the material they have heard. This advantageous program provides children with many learning opportunities as well. They get perspective through character and plot development. They make inferences about the story and what will happen next through oral practice. This type of practice is crucial in their learning. Additionally, when they evaluate the literature, it satisfies the children's learning development and growth. The emotional and mental development of these young children is nurtured and fostered as their minds grow and develop into more complex ways of thinking. Books have the power to transform anyone into anything he or she wants to be and aid a person's success. Indeed, these pre-schoolers are first in line for a journey of a lifetime when they can be a part of such a favorable program as story time.

Finally, children aren't the only ones valuing the excellence of these programs; parents benefit as well. They can relax and watch the story-telling from cushioned chairs in the same room as their children, or they can opt to sit on the floor beside them. This program is also useful for parents to get ideas for their own home story-telling sessions. Whether they enjoy the different voices the story-teller reads or the prop ideas or endless book lists, parents can surely find new ideas to incorporate at home. Moreover, parents can be a part of their children's development and growth process. They can see the knowledge pouring into their children's brain, one book at a time, if they look closely enough. A child's learning opportunity is the most invaluable experience parents and their children share with one another, and pre-school story time is the best way parents and children can interact with one another through books and story-telling.

Overall, pre-school story time is an exceptional literature program that fosters a child's learning development. It expands a child's knowledge through learning opportunities and provides a friendly atmosphere that calls for a child to have fun. Parents can even participate with their children in this program. This is truly the choice program for pre-schoolers. Parents, take your child to story time at the public library.

KARLA ROBERTS

Walden's Pond Stable

Karla Roberts is earning an Associate of Science degree with an emphasis in pre-veterinarian medicine. She plans to complete the veterinarian program at CSU-Fort Collins and work as a large animal vet. In the past two years, she has been recognized by the Arts and Sciences Division as an outstanding student in English, biology and trigonometry.

Walking down a dusty aisle, I see particles of dust dance in the slits of sunlight coming through the windows. The warm smell of hay and shaving fill my senses and make me feel at home. Moving to the door at the end of the stable, I feel my excitement start to rise because I'm going to see my best friend. As I open the door, the rough wood slides under my hand, and I'm immediately greeted by a happy whinny from the occupant inside the stall. I answer back by feeding my oldest horse an apple and rubbing his nose. As I lead my horse from his stall, I take in the beautiful sight of Walden's Pond Stable. The stable is located in Mechanicsville, Virginia, a town sweetened by southern charm, where I've boarded my horses for the last four years. The beautiful barn, the accommodations, and the people make Walden's Pond Stable an enjoyable and often entertaining place to board my horses.

One of my favorite features of Walden's Pond Stable is the beautiful barn and pastures. Set on forty acres of land, the barn is shaped like an old chapel with high ceilings and wide aisles. It gives the impression of a comfortable, lived-in home. Adding to this impression is the fact that the barn is made completely of wood. Newer stables made out of steel and tin may seem stronger than a wooden barn, but Walden's Stable has been standing for fifty years and is still the rock it was when it was first built. The stalls are also built of a warm mahogany wood with easy sliding doors making the stable not only charming but also easy to work in. There are also wide windows in all the stalls. These windows let clear, bright light shine in early mornings, and a warm yellow light glows radiantly during the evenings. Along with the charming stable are the forty acres of lush green rolling pastures that are heavenly to any horse, and my horses are no different. Altogether there are six pastures, each with its own appeal. My favorite pasture, however, is the one that is the stable's namesake, Walden's Pond. The pasture has a small but deep pond, a favorite spot for many horses as they can take a dip in the cool water on sticky, hot summer days.

Another reason I enjoy Walden's Pond Stable, besides the charming barn and grounds, is the accommodations offered for the horses boarded at the stable. Walden's Pond has staff to feed and turn out the horses in the morning. This is a real blessing for me since I'm not a morning person. There is also plenty of space to store horse equipment and supplies, such as the spacious tack room with hangers for saddles and bridles and a hay loft upstairs. Another convenience is the shavings bins for easy access to clean shavings for the stalls. Equally important are the larger than average sized stalls where any breed of horse can easily fit. My draft horse that stands seventeen hands high and weighs two thousand pounds would not be able to fit in a normal size stall, so boarding my horse at Walden's Stable has been great. Along with the accommodations in the barn, there are also special pastures just for miniature horses boarded at the stable. These pastures have fencing that is only waist high so smaller horses can see everyone but don't have to be out with the big horses where they could be injured. For the larger horses, there are spacious pastures with strong fencing where the horses can enjoy being out and the owners won't have to worry about their horses getting loose.

Even with the lovely barn and the considerable accommodations, it's the interesting people at Walden's Pond Stable who make it my favorite place to be. One of the most interesting people at Walden's Stable is Regina, the barn's "watch dog." She can always be found prowling up and down the aisles, giving unsolicited advice to unsuspecting stray boarders. When I first came to board my horses at Walden's Stable, Regina was a bit overwhelming. She showed me how to hang a water bucket in a stall and the proper way to turn on a hose, but as time passed, I began to value her opinion. The knowledge and experience I gained from my time with her was immeasurable. One time a horse at the stable became ill from eating too much grain, and Regina knew just what to do to keep the horse going until a vet could arrive. Another character at the stable is Dora, a horse trainer and riding instructor. She is the sweetest and least imposing person I know, but when working with horses or instructing riders, she is all business. When taking riding lessons from Dora, a student is never allowed to say he or she can't do something. This can seem a challenging way to learn, but it pushes a student to do better than even she thought she could. One of my greatest fears was cantering on a horse because of a bad fall I had in the past. It was with Dora's instruction that I overcame my fear and started to enjoy riding again.

Although there are many places to board horses, not many stables have so many positive aspects to them. The beautiful stable and pastures, the wonderful accommodations, and the array of interesting boarders make Walden's Pond Stable a place I would recommend to any horse owner. This is not just a fantastic place for an owner to board his or her horses but also a place that can become a second home.

JARED BROWN

Eminem's Incredible Skill as a Song Writer

Jared Brown competed in public speaking competitions at the national level in high school. After attending PCC, he plans to transfer to Colorado State University Pueblo to earn a BSN degree in nursing. Eventually, he hopes to complete a graduate nursing degree.

Would you ever have guessed that a so-called "introverted child," growing up in an abusive home, raised by a drug-addicted, single mother, would one day emerge from a cut-throat ghetto to be the most talented musical artist of our time? If you answered no, you are not alone. The majority of individuals in Marshall Mathers' life did not see his potential either. However, because of his incredible determination and unparalleled natural talent, young Marshall soon became what many call the most talented hip-hop writer of all time, known as Eminem.

Eminem possesses a magnetic quality that has gained the respect of so many critics, rival rappers, and even those who dislike the Hip-Hop genre altogether, creating intrigue in a way that few can explain. The reason for this respect is the incredible amount of depth in Marshall Mathers' writing ability. The first and most prominent skill of this particular artist is the ability to tell a story in a way which is so clear that it paints a visual portrait in the listeners' minds. These relatable stories are combined with a firm grasp of sound in the English language to add another colorful level dabbed on his lyrical canvas. Although these traits have already separated Eminem from most artists, it is his deep penetration into the meaning of his chosen words that is the finishing stoke on each of his masterpieces.

The power to narrate a story well is a gift people always have admired. It is also something seldom found in the rap subculture. This is the reason so many unsatisfied listeners spin the radio dial as soon as they hear the unmistakable beats of this genre. Many simply cannot relate to the posturing of gangsters and want something more. That "something" is exactly what Eminem provides. It is easy to relate to and feel the same emotion which Mathers conveys, whether or not a person has grown up in the environment that he experienced and expresses in his songs. The fact that he is not trying to "prove himself" allows Eminem to express feelings such as sadness, weakness, or even love for his daughter. These feelings will never be detected in the music of the average rapper who is desperately trying to maintain a "tough-guy" persona.

Of course, it takes more than a good story to make an impression in the world of rap, and this is where Mathers exhibits his unparalleled knowledge of lingual sound and rhythm. It was his rhyming style which revolutionized the structure of rap. Before Eminem there were two predominant rhyming styles: one consisted of the last words of the verses rhyming with each other, and the other style included the first *and* the middle word in each line rhyming with the next. However, Marshal Mathers would not be limited by these constricting lyrical guidelines. One of his first displays of a new style can be found in his famous song "Lose Yourself," released in 2002. In the first minute and a half of this song, leading to the chorus, there is scarcely a single word that does not rhyme or have a matching vowel sound with another. Not only do the rhymes work flawlessly together, but the way each sound is placed in the sentence seems to form a beat all its own. It is a jaw-dropping example of this artist's skill in writing.

While maintaining this unceasing rhyming cadence, combined with effective and relatable narration, this young, ordinary-looking artist deploys one more lyrical power. It is his ability to manipulate the meaning of words to form a sub-theme in his lyrics. Using words with particular imagery attached can form a message subliminally carried through a verse. This talent is best explained with examples. In the song "No Love," referring to those people who have tried to hold him back, Eminem says, "You will be roasted, because Marshal's not mellow." When first listening to this, one may miss the subliminal picture of a "roasted marshmallow," which is cleverly placed in midst of a fast-paced song. Another example of this is his line written in 2011: "...there is too much at stake, when you find someone this raw, with a beat this rare." By placing a homophone of the word "steak" followed by the adjectives "raw" and "rare," it is clear what lyrical theme he is developing. These secondary meanings may not even pertain to the external subject of the song, but they do act, in a way, as the extra glint on his crown and a way for the artist to show off a deeper level of skill.

Whether a person is a lover of Rap music or is one who believes that the genre is frequently destructive to society, it is impossible to honestly deny the immense natural talent and insight possessed by the young man with the dysfunctional past—a man with the ability to gain the respect of so many who dislike him. Perhaps this is because of the retreat he offers from the posturing, superficial, "gangster-rap," with his emotional life-experiences. Maybe it is the clever plays on words that tickle the mind or possibly the skill he displays in rhyming and rhythm. We may never know the true reason for the intrigue he creates, but we do know it will make us remove our hand from the radio dial the next time his songs begin to play.

DAVID BRUCK   [b. 1949]

The Death Penalty

David Bruck is a graduate of Harvard College and the University of
South Carolina Law School. Practicing criminal law since 1976, Bruck
has dedicated his practice almost exclusively to the defense of those
accused of capital crimes. Having served as both the Richland County
public defender and as chief attorney of the South Carolina Office of
Appellate Defense, Bruck is now director of the Virginia Capital Case
Clearinghouse, a capital trial defense clinic and resource center at
Washington & Lee Law School, where he is also a faculty member. He
has successfully argued a number of high-profile death penalty cases,
including that of *State v. Susan Smith*, a mother accused of drowning
her two children. Bruck has testified before U.S. Congressional com-
mittees on death penalty legislation and was honored in 1996 with the
John Minor Wisdom Public Service & Professionalism Award from the
American Bar Association.

Bruck's piece "The Death Penalty," originally published in 1985 in
The New Republic, is a response to New York City Mayor Ed Koch's
assertion that enforcing the death penalty demonstrates society's commitment to recognize the "value of the victim's life." Bruck does not
advocate the death penalty, citing cases of mistaken identity, inadequate legal representation on the part of the condemned, prejudicial
juries, and the futility of executing the mentally ill. Bruck's true concern lies with the celebrity attached to the death-row inmate, the press
coverage that both sensationalizes the case and condones a jeering
public's shameless applause at the execution.

Mayor Ed Koch contends that the death penalty "affirms life." By failing
to execute murderers, he says, we "signal a lessened regard for the value
of the victim's life." Koch suggests that people who oppose the death
penalty are like Kitty Genovese's neighbors, who heard her cries for help
but did nothing while an attacker stabbed her to death.

This is the standard "moral" defense of death as punishment: Even if executions don't deter violent crime any more effectively than imprisonment,

David Bruck, "The Death Penalty" from *The New Republic,* May 20, 1985. Copyright
© 1985 by The New Republic, Inc. Reprinted by permission of The New Republic.

49

they are still required as the only means we have of doing justice in response to the worst of crimes.

Until recently, this "moral" argument had to be considered in the abstract, since no one was being executed in the United States. But the death penalty is back now, at least in the southern states, where every one of the more than thirty executions carried out over the last two years has taken place. Those of us who live in those states are getting to see the difference between the death penalty in theory, and what happens when you actually try to use it.

South Carolina resumed executing prisoners in January with the electrocution of Joseph Carl Shaw. Shaw was condemned to death for helping to murder two teenagers while he was serving as a military policeman at Fort Jackson, South Carolina. His crime, propelled by mental illness and PCP, was one of terrible brutality. It is Shaw's last words ("Killing was wrong when I did it. It is wrong when you do it. . . .") that so outraged Mayor Koch: He finds it "a curiosity of modern life that we are being lectured on morality by cold-blooded killers." And so it is.

But it was not "modern life" that brought this curiosity into being. 5 It was capital punishment. The electric chair was J. C. Shaw's platform. (The mayor mistakenly writes that Shaw's statement came in the form of a plea to the governor for clemency: Actually Shaw made it only seconds before his death, as he waited, shaved and strapped into the chair, for the switch to be thrown.) It was the chair that provided Shaw with celebrity and an opportunity to lecture us on right and wrong. What made this weird moral reversal even worse is that J. C. Shaw faced his own death with undeniable dignity and courage. And while Shaw died, the TV crews recorded another "curiosity" of the death penalty — the crowd gathered outside the death-house to cheer on the executioner. Whoops of elation greeted the announcement of Shaw's death. Waiting at the penitentiary gates for the appearance of the hearse bearing Shaw's remains, one demonstrator started yelling, "Where's the beef?"

For those who had to see the execution of J. C. Shaw, it wasn't easy to keep in mind that the purpose of the whole spectacle was to affirm life. It will be harder still when Florida executes a cop-killer named Alvin Ford. Ford has lost his mind during his years of death-row confinement, and now spends his days trembling, rocking back and forth, and muttering unintelligible prayers. This has led to litigation over whether Ford meets a centuries-old legal standard for mental competency. Since the Middle Ages, the Anglo-American legal system has generally prohibited the execution of anyone who is too mentally ill to understand what is about to be done to him and why. If Florida wins its case, it will have earned the right to electrocute Ford in his present condition. If it loses, he will not be executed until the state has first nursed him back to some semblance of mental health.°

We can at least be thankful that this demoralizing spectacle involves a prisoner who is actually guilty of murder. But this may not always be so. The ordeal of Lenell Jeter—the young black engineer who recently served more than a year of a life sentence for a Texas armed robbery that he didn't commit—should remind us that the system is quite capable of making the very worst sort of mistake. That Jeter was eventually cleared is a fluke. If the robbery had occurred at 7 P.M. rather than 3 P.M., he'd have had no alibi, and would still be in prison today. And if someone had been killed in that robbery, Jeter probably would have been sentenced to death. We'd have seen the usual execution-day interviews with state officials and the victim's relatives, all complaining that Jeter's appeals took too long. And Jeter's last words from the gurney would have taken their place among the growing literature of death-house oration that so irritates the mayor.

Koch quotes Hugo Adam Bedau, a prominent abolitionist, to the effect that the record fails to establish that innocent defendants have been executed in the past. But this doesn't mean, as Koch implies, that it hasn't happened. All Bedau was saying was that doubts concerning executed prisoners' guilt are almost never resolved. Bedau is at work now on an effort to determine how many wrongful death sentences may have been imposed: His list of murder convictions since 1900 in which the state eventually *admitted* error is some four hundred cases long. Of course, very few of these cases involved actual executions: The mistakes that Bedau documents were uncovered precisely because the prisoner was alive and able to fight for his vindication. The cases where someone is executed are the very cases in which we're least likely to learn that we got the wrong man.

I don't claim that executions of entirely innocent people will occur very often. But they will occur. And other sorts of mistakes already have. Roosevelt Green was executed in Georgia two days before J. C. Shaw. Green and an accomplice kidnapped a young woman. Green swore that his companion shot her to death after Green had left, and that he knew nothing about the murder. Green's claim was supported by a statement that his accomplice made to a witness after the crime. The jury never

---

Alvin Ford case: Florida lost its case to execute Ford. On June 26, 1986, the U.S. Supreme Court ruled that the execution of an insane person violates the Eighth Amendment, which forbids cruel and unusual punishments. Therefore, convicted murderers cannot be executed if they have become so insane that they do not know that they are about to be executed and do not understand the reason for their sentence. If Ford regains his sanity, however, he can be executed.

resolved whether Green was telling the truth, and when he tried to take a polygraph examination a few days before his scheduled execution, the state of Georgia refused to allow the examiner into the prison. As the pressure for symbolic retribution mounts, the courts, like the public, are losing patience with such details. Green was electrocuted on January 9, while members of the Ku Klux Klan rallied outside the prison.

Then there is another sort of arbitrariness that happens all the time. 10 Last October, Louisiana executed a man named Ernest Knighton. Knighton had killed a gas station owner during a robbery. Like any murder, this was a terrible crime. But it was not premeditated, and is the sort of crime that very rarely results in a death sentence. Why was Knighton electrocuted when almost everyone else who committed the same offense was not? Was it because he was black? Was it because his victim and all twelve members of the jury that sentenced him were white? Was it because Knighton's court-appointed lawyer presented no evidence on his behalf at his sentencing hearing? Or maybe there's no reason except bad luck. One thing is clear: Ernest Knighton was picked out to die the way a fisherman takes a cricket out of a bait jar. No one cares which cricket gets impaled on the hook.

Not every prisoner executed recently was chosen that randomly. But many were. And having selected these men so casually, so blindly, the death penalty system asks us to accept that the purpose of killing each of them is to affirm the sanctity of human life.

The death penalty states are also learning that the death penalty is easier to advocate than it is to administer. In Florida, where executions have become almost routine, the governor reports that nearly a third of his time is spent reviewing the clemency requests of condemned prisoners. The Florida Supreme Court is hopelessly backlogged with death cases. Some have taken five years to decide, and the rest of the Court's work waits in line behind the death appeals. Florida's death row currently holds more than 230 prisoners. State officials are reportedly considering building a special "death prison" devoted entirely to the isolation and electrocution of the condemned. The state is also considering the creation of a special public defender unit that will do nothing else but handle death penalty appeals. The death penalty, in short, is spawning death agencies.

And what is Florida getting for all of this? The state went through almost all of 1983 without executing anyone: Its rate of intentional homicide declined by 17 percent. Last year Florida executed eight people—the most of any state, and the sixth highest total for any year since Florida started electrocuting people back in 1924. Elsewhere in the United States last year, the homicide rate continued to decline. But in Florida, it actually rose by 5.1 percent.

But these are just the tiresome facts. The electric chair has been a centerpiece of each of Koch's recent political campaigns, and he knows better than anyone how little the facts have to do with the public's support for capital punishment. What really fuels the death penalty is the justifiable frustration and rage of people who see that the government is not coping with violent crime. So what if the death penalty doesn't work? At least it gives us the satisfaction of knowing that we got one or two of the sons of bitches.

Perhaps we want retribution on the flesh and bone of a handful of con-   15
victed murderers so badly that we're willing to close our eyes to all of the demoralization and danger that come with it. A lot of politicians think so, and they may be right. But if they are, then let's at least look honestly at what we're doing. This lottery of death both comes from and encourages an attitude toward human life that is not reverent, but reckless.

And that is why the mayor is dead wrong when he confuses such fury with justice. He suggests that we trivialize murder unless we kill murderers. By that logic, we also trivialize rape unless we sodomize rapists. The sin of Kitty Genovese's neighbors wasn't that they failed to stab her attacker to death. Justice does demand that murderers be punished. And common sense demands that society be protected from them. But neither justice nor self-preservation demands that we kill men whom we have already imprisoned.

The electric chair in which J. C. Shaw died earlier this year was built in 1912 at the suggestion of South Carolina's governor at the time, Cole Blease. Governor Blease's other criminal justice initiative was an impassioned crusade in favor of lynch law. Any lesser response, the governor insisted, trivialized the loathsome crimes of interracial rape and murder. In 1912, a lot of people agreed with Governor Blease that a proper regard for justice required both lynching and the electric chair. Eventually we are going to learn that justice requires neither.

53

MARTIN LUTHER KING JR. [1929–1968]

Letter from Birmingham Jail

The foremost leader of the American civil rights movement of the 1950s and 1960s, **Martin Luther King Jr.** was born in Atlanta, Georgia, in 1929 and assassinated in Memphis, Tennessee, in 1968. He was an ordained minister with a Ph.D., a deliverer of powerful sermons and speeches, and a writer of books. A crusader against segregation, an organizer of the Montgomery, Alabama, bus boycott, and head of the Southern Christian Leadership Conference, King advocated nonviolent resistance in the face of discrimination and violence. The steadfast dignity with which he pursued rights for African Americans earned him worldwide renown and a Nobel Peace Prize.

"Letter from Birmingham Jail" was written while King and hundreds of other protesters were under arrest for demonstrating in Birmingham, Alabama. It is a response to eight of his fellow clergymen who questioned his methods of protest even as they supported his ultimate aims. Note, as you read, the combination in his writing of the cool logic of his argument and his passionate sense of the injustice African Americans have suffered.

MY DEAR FELLOW CLERGYMEN:

While confined here in the Birmingham city jail, I came across your recent statement calling my present activities "unwise and untimely." Seldom do I pause to answer criticism of my work and ideas. If I sought to answer all the criticisms that cross my desk, my secretaries would have little time for anything other than such correspondence in the course of the day, and I would have no time for constructive work. But since I feel that you are men of genuine good will and that your criticisms are sincerely set forth, I want to try to answer your statement in what I hope will be patient and reasonable terms.

I think I should indicate why I am here in Birmingham, since you have been influenced by the view which argues against "outsiders coming in." I have the honor of serving as president of the Southern Christian Leadership Conference, an organization operating in every southern state, with headquarters in Atlanta, Georgia. We have some eighty-five affiliated organizations across the South, and one of them is the Alabama Christian Movement for Human Rights. Frequently we share staff, educational, and financial resources with our affiliates. Several months ago the affiliate here in Birmingham asked us to be on call to engage in a nonviolent direct-action program if such were deemed necessary. We readily consented, and when the hour came we lived up to our promise. So I, along with several members of my staff, am here because I was invited here. I am here because I have organizational ties here.

But more basically, I am in Birmingham because injustice is here. Just as the prophets of the eighth century B.C. left their villages and carried their "thus saith the Lord" far beyond the boundaries of their home towns, and just as the Apostle Paul left his village of Tarsus and carried the gospel of Jesus Christ to the far corners of the Greco-Roman world, so am I compelled to carry the gospel of freedom beyond my own home town. Like Paul, I must constantly respond to the Macedonian call for aid.

Moreover, I am cognizant of the interrelatedness of all communities and states. I cannot sit idly by in Atlanta and not be concerned about what happens in Birmingham. Injustice anywhere is a threat to justice everywhere. We are caught in an inescapable network of mutuality, tied in a single garment of destiny. Whatever affects one directly, affects all indirectly. Never again can we afford to live with the narrow, provincial "outside agitator" idea. Anyone who lives inside the United States can never be considered an outsider anywhere within its bounds.

You deplore the demonstrations taking place in Birmingham. But 5 your statement, I am sorry to say, fails to express a similar concern for the conditions that brought about the demonstrations. I am sure that none of you would want to rest content with the superficial kind of social analysis that deals merely with effects and does not grapple with underlying causes. It is unfortunate that demonstrations are taking place in Birmingham, but it is even more unfortunate that the city's white power structure left the Negro community with no alternative.

In any nonviolent campaign there are four basic steps: collection of the facts to determine whether injustices exist; negotiation; self-purification; and direct action. We have gone through all these steps in Birmingham. There can be no gainsaying the fact that racial injustice engulfs this community. Birmingham is probably the most thoroughly segregated city in the United States. Its ugly record of brutality is widely known. Negroes have experienced grossly unjust treatment in the courts. There have been more unsolved bombings of Negro homes and churches in Birmingham than in any other city in the nation. These are the hard, brutal facts of the case. On the basis of these conditions, Negro leaders

55

sought to negotiate with the city fathers. But the latter consistently re-fused to engage in good-faith negotiation.

Then, last September, came the opportunity to talk with leaders of Birmingham's economic community. In the course of the negotiations, certain promises were made by the merchants—for example, to remove the stores' humiliating racial signs. On the basis of these promises, the Reverend Fred Shuttlesworth and the leaders of the Alabama Christian Movement for Human Rights agreed to a moratorium on all demonstra-tions. As the weeks and months went by, we realized that we were the victims of a broken promise. A few signs, briefly removed, returned; the others remained.

As in so many past experiences, our hopes had been blasted, and the shadow of deep disappointment settled upon us. We had no alternative except to prepare for direct action, whereby we would present our very bodies as a means of laying our case before the conscience of the local and the national community. Mindful of the difficulties involved, we de-cided to undertake a process of self-purification. We began a series of workshops on nonviolence, and we repeatedly asked ourselves: "Are you able to accept blows without retaliating?" "Are you able to endure the or-deal of jail?" We decided to schedule our direct-action program for the Easter season, realizing that except for Christmas, this is the main shop-ping period of the year. Knowing that a strong economic withdrawal program would be the by-product of direct action, we felt that this would be the best time to bring pressure to bear on the merchants for the needed change.

Then it occurred to us that Birmingham's mayoral election was com-ing up in March, and we speedily decided to postpone action until after election day. When we discovered that the Commissioner of Public Safety, Eugene "Bull" Connor, had piled up enough votes to be in the run-off, we decided again to postpone action until the day after the runoff so that the demonstrations could not be used to cloud the issues. Like many others, we wanted to see Mr. Connor defeated, and to this end we endured postponement after postponement. Having aided in this community need, we felt that our direct-action program could be de-layed no longer.

You may well ask, "Why direct action? Why sit-ins, marches, and so 10 forth? Isn't negotiation a better path?" You are quite right in calling for negotiation. Indeed, this is the very purpose of direct action. Nonviolent direct action seeks to create such a crisis and foster such a tension that a community which has constantly refused to negotiate is forced to con-front the issue. It seeks so to dramatize the issue that it can no longer be ignored. My citing the creation of tension as part of the work of the nonviolent-resister may sound rather shocking. But I must confess that I am not afraid of the word "tension." I have earnestly opposed violent tension, but there is a type of constructive, nonviolent tension which is necessary for growth. Just as Socrates felt that it was necessary to create a tension in the mind so that individuals could rise from the bondage of myths and half-truths to the unfettered realm of creative analysis and objective appraisal, so must we see the need for nonviolent gadflies to create the kind of tension in society that will help men rise from the dark depths of prejudice and racism to the majestic heights of understanding and brotherhood.

The purpose of our direct-action program is to create a situation so crisis-packed that it will inevitably open the door to negotiation. I therefore concur with you in your call for negotiation. Too long has our beloved Southland been bogged down in a tragic effort to live in monologue rather than dialogue.

One of the basic points in your statement is that the action that I and my associates have taken in Birmingham is untimely. Some have asked: "Why didn't you give the new city administration time to act?" The only answer that I can give to this query is that the new Birmingham administration must be prodded about as much as the outgoing one, before it will act. We are sadly mistaken if we feel that the election of Albert Boutwell as mayor will bring the millennium to Birmingham. While Mr. Boutwell is a much more gentle person than Mr. Connor, they are both segregationists, dedicated to maintenance of the status quo. I have hoped that Mr. Boutwell will be reasonable enough to see the futility of massive resistance to desegregation. But he will not see this without pressure from devotees of civil rights. My friends, I must say to you that we have not made a single gain in civil rights without determined legal and nonviolent pressure. Lamentably, it is an historical fact that privileged groups seldom give up their privileges voluntarily. Individuals may see the moral light and voluntarily give up their unjust posture, but, as Reinhold Niebuhr has reminded us, groups tend to be more immoral than individuals.

We know through painful experience that freedom is never voluntarily given by the oppressor; it must be demanded by the oppressed. Frankly, I have yet to engage in a direct-action campaign that was "well timed" in the view of those who have not suffered unduly from the disease of segregation. For years now I have heard the word "Wait!" It rings in the ear of every Negro with piercing familiarity. This "Wait" has almost always meant "Never." We must come to see, with one of our distinguished jurists, that "justice too long delayed is justice denied."

We have waited for more than 340 years for our constitutional and God-given rights. The nations of Asia and Africa are moving with jet-like speed toward gaining political independence, but we still creep at horse-

and-buggy pace toward gaining a cup of coffee at a lunch counter. Perhaps it is easy for those who have never felt the stinging darts of segregation to say, "Wait." But when you have seen vicious mobs lynch your mothers and fathers at will and drown your sisters and brothers at whim; when you have seen hate-filled policemen curse, kick, and even kill your black brothers and sisters; when you see the vast majority of your twenty million Negro brothers smothering in an airtight cage of poverty in the midst of an affluent society; when you suddenly find your tongue twisted and your speech stammering as you seek to explain to your six-year-old daughter why she can't go to the public amusement park that has just been advertised on television, and see tears welling up in her eyes when she is told that Funtown is closed to colored children, and see ominous clouds of inferiority beginning to form in her little mental sky, and see her beginning to distort her personality by developing an unconscious bitterness toward white people; when you have to concoct an answer for a five-year-old son who is asking, "Daddy, why do white people treat colored people so mean?"; when you take a cross-country drive and find it necessary to sleep night after night in the uncomfortable corners of your automobile because no motel will accept you; when you are humiliated day in and day out by nagging signs reading "white" and "colored"; when your first name becomes "nigger," your middle name becomes "boy" (however old you are) and your last name becomes "John," and your wife and mother are never given the respected title "Mrs."; when you are harried by day and haunted by night by the fact that you are a Negro, living constantly at tiptoe stance, never quite knowing what to expect next, and are plagued with inner fears and outer resentments; when you are forever fighting a degenerating sense of "nobodiness" — then you will understand why we find it difficult to wait. There comes a time when the cup of endurance runs over, and men are no longer willing to be plunged into the abyss of despair. I hope, sirs, you can understand our legitimate and unavoidable impatience.

You express a great deal of anxiety over our willingness to break laws. 15 This is certainly a legitimate concern. Since we so diligently urge people to obey the Supreme Court's decision of 1954 outlawing segregation in the public schools, at first glance it may seem rather paradoxical for us consciously to break laws. One may well ask: "How can you advocate breaking some laws and obeying others?" The answer lies in the fact that there are two types of laws: just and unjust. I would be the first to advocate obeying just laws. One has not only a legal but a moral responsibility to obey just laws. Conversely, one has a moral responsibility to disobey unjust laws. I would agree with St. Augustine that "an unjust law is no law at all."

Now, what is the difference between the two? How does one determine whether a law is just or unjust? A just law is a man-made code that squares with the moral law or the law of God. An unjust law is a code that is out of harmony with the moral law. To put it in the terms of St. Thomas Aquinas: An unjust law is a human law that is not rooted in eternal law and natural law. Any law that uplifts human personality is just. Any law that degrades human personality is unjust. All segregation statutes are unjust because segregation distorts the soul and damages the personality. It gives the segregator a false sense of superiority and the segregated a false sense of inferiority. Segregation, to use the terminology of the Jewish philosopher Martin Buber, substitutes an "I-it" relationship for an "I-thou" relationship and ends up relegating persons to the status of things. Hence segregation is not only politically, economically, and sociologically unsound, it is morally wrong and sinful. Paul Tillich has said that sin is separation. Is not segregation an existential expression of man's tragic separation, his awful estrangement, his terrible sinfulness? Thus it is that I can urge men to obey the 1954 decision of the Supreme Court, for it is morally right; and I can urge them to disobey segregation ordinances, for they are morally wrong.

Let us consider a more concrete example of just and unjust laws. An unjust law is a code that a numerical or power majority group compels a minority group to obey but does not make binding on itself. This is *difference* made legal. By the same token, a just law is a code that a majority compels a minority to follow and that it is willing to follow itself. This is *sameness* made legal.

Let me give another explanation. A law is unjust if it is inflicted on a minority that, as a result of being denied the right to vote, had no part in enacting or devising the law. Who can say that the legislature of Alabama which set up that state's segregation laws was democratically elected? Throughout Alabama all sorts of devious methods are used to prevent Negroes from becoming registered voters, and there are some counties in which, even though Negroes constitute a majority of the population, not a single Negro is registered. Can any law enacted under such circumstances be considered democratically structured?

Sometimes a law is just on its face and unjust in its application. For instance, I have been arrested on a charge of parading without a permit. Now, there is nothing wrong in having an ordinance which requires a permit for a parade. But such an ordinance becomes unjust when it is used to maintain segregation and to deny citizens the First-Amendment privilege of peaceful assembly and protest.

I hope you are able to see the distinction I am trying to point out. In 20 no sense do I advocate evading or defying the law, as would the rabid segregationist. That would lead to anarchy. One who breaks an unjust law must do so openly, lovingly, and with a willingness to accept the penalty. I submit that an individual who breaks a law that conscience tells him is unjust, and who willingly accepts the penalty of imprisonment in order to arouse the conscience of the community over its injustice, is in reality expressing the highest respect for law.

Of course, there is nothing new about this kind of civil disobedience. It was evidenced sublimely in the refusal of Shadrach, Meshach, and Abednego to obey the laws of Nebuchadnezzar, on the ground that a higher moral law was at stake. It was practiced superbly by the early Christians, who were willing to face hungry lions and the excruciating pain of chopping blocks rather than submit to certain unjust laws of the Roman Empire. To a degree, academic freedom is a reality today because Socrates practiced civil disobedience. In our own nation, the Boston Tea Party represented a massive act of civil disobedience.

We should never forget that everything Adolf Hitler did in Germany was "legal" and everything the Hungarian freedom fighters did in Hungary was "illegal." It was "illegal" to aid and comfort a Jew in Hitler's Germany. Even so, I am sure that, had I lived in Germany at the time, I would have aided and comforted my Jewish brothers. If today I lived in a Communist country where certain principles dear to the Christian faith are suppressed, I would openly advocate disobeying that country's antireligious laws.

I must make two honest confessions to you, my Christian and Jewish brothers. First, I must confess that over the past few years I have been gravely disappointed with the white moderate. I have almost reached the regrettable conclusion that the Negro's great stumbling block in his stride toward freedom is not the White Citizen's Counciler or the Ku Klux Klanner, but the white moderate, who is more devoted to "order" than to justice; who prefers a negative peace which is the absence of tension to a positive peace which is the presence of justice; who constantly says, "I agree with you in the goal you seek, but I cannot agree with your methods of direct action"; who paternalistically believes he can set the timetable for another man's freedom; who lives by a mythical concept of time and who constantly advises the Negro to wait for a "more convenient season." Shallow understanding from people of good will is more frustrating than absolute misunderstanding from people of ill will. Lukewarm acceptance is much more bewildering than outright rejection.

I had hoped that the white moderate would understand that law and order exist for the purpose of establishing justice and that when they fail in this purpose they become the dangerously structured dams that block the flow of social progress. I had hoped that the white moderate would understand that the present tension in the South is a necessary phase of the transition from an obnoxious negative peace, in which the Negro passively accepted his unjust plight, to a substantive and positive peace, in which all men will respect the dignity and worth of human personality. Actually, we who engage in nonviolent direct action are not the creators of tension. We merely bring to the surface the hidden tension that is already alive. We bring it out in the open, where it can be seen and dealt with. Like a boil that can never be cured so long as it is covered up but must be opened with all its ugliness to the natural medicines of air and light, injustice must be exposed, with all the tension its exposure creates, to the light of human conscience and the air of national opinion, before it can be cured.

In your statement you assert that our actions, even though peaceful, 25 must be condemned because they precipitate violence. But is this a logical assertion? Isn't this like condemning a robbed man because his possession of money precipitated the evil act of robbery? Isn't this like condemning Socrates because his unswerving commitment to truth and his philosophical inquiries precipitated the act by the misguided populace in which they made him drink hemlock? Isn't this like condemning Jesus because his unique God-consciousness and never-ceasing devotion to God's will precipitated the evil act of crucifixion? We must come to see that, as the federal courts have consistently affirmed, it is wrong to urge an individual to cease his efforts to gain his basic constitutional rights because the quest may precipitate violence. Society must protect the robbed and punish the robber.

I had also hoped that the white moderate would reject the myth concerning time in relation to the struggle for freedom. I have just received a letter from a white brother in Texas. He writes: "All Christians know that the colored people will receive equal rights eventually, but it is possible that you are in too great a religious hurry. It has taken Christianity almost two thousand years to accomplish what it has. The teachings of Christ take time to come to earth." Such an attitude stems from a tragic misconception of time, from the strangely irrational notion that there is something in the very flow of time that will inevitably cure all ills. Actually, time itself is neutral; it can be used either destructively or constructively. More and more I feel that the people of ill will have used time much more effectively than have the people of good will. We will have to repent in this generation not merely for the hateful words and actions of the bad people, but for the appalling silence of the good people. Human progress never rolls in on wheels of inevitability; it comes through the tireless efforts of men willing to be co-workers with God, and without this hard work, time itself becomes an ally of the forces of social stagnation. We must use time creatively, in the knowledge that the time is always ripe to do right. Now is the time to make real the promise of democracy and transform our pending national elegy into a creative psalm of brotherhood. Now is the time to lift our national policy from the quicksand of racial injustice to the solid rock of human dignity.

You speak of our activity in Birmingham as extreme. At first I was rather disappointed that fellow clergymen would see my nonviolent efforts as those of an extremist. I began thinking about the fact that I stand in the middle of two opposing forces in the Negro community. One is a force of complacency, made up in part of Negroes who, as a result of long years of oppression, are so drained of self-respect and a sense of "somebodiness" that they have adjusted to segregation; and in part of a few middle-class Negroes who, because of a degree of academic and economic security and because in some ways they profit by segregation, have become insensitive to the problems of the masses. The other force is one of bitterness and hatred, and it comes perilously close to advocating violence. It is expressed in the various black nationalist groups that are springing up across the nation, the largest and best-known being Elijah Muhammad's Muslim movement. Nourished by the Negro's frustration over the continued existence of racial discrimination, this movement is made up of people who have lost faith in America, who have absolutely repudiated Christianity, and who have concluded that the white man is an incorrigible "devil."

I have tried to stand between these two forces, saying that we need emulate neither the "do-nothingism" of the complacent nor the hatred and despair of the black nationalist. For there is the more excellent way of love and nonviolent protest. I am grateful to God that, through the influence of the Negro church, the way of nonviolence became an integral part of our struggle.

If this philosophy had not emerged, by now many streets of the South would, I am convinced, be flowing with blood. And I am further convinced that if our white brothers dismiss as "rabblerousers" and "outside agitators" those of us who employ nonviolent direct action, and if they refuse to support our nonviolent efforts, millions of Negroes will, out of frustration and despair, seek solace and security in black-nationalist ideologies—a development that would inevitably lead to a frightening racial nightmare.

Oppressed people cannot remain oppressed forever. The yearning for 30 freedom eventually manifests itself, and that is what has happened to the American Negro. Something within has reminded him of his birthright of freedom, and something without has reminded him that it can be gained. Consciously or unconsciously, he has been caught up by the *Zeitgeist*, and with his black brothers of Africa and his brown and yellow brothers of Asia, South America, and the Caribbean, the United States Negro is moving with a sense of great urgency toward the promised land of racial justice. If one recognizes this vital urge that has engulfed the Negro community, one should readily understand why public demonstrations are taking place. The Negro has many pent-up resentments and latent frustrations, and he must release them. So let him march; let him make prayer pilgrimages to the city hall; let him go on freedom rides—and try to understand why he must do so. If his repressed emotions are not released in nonviolent ways, they will seek expression through violence; this is not a threat but a fact of history. So I have not said to my people, "Get rid of your discontent." Rather, I have tried to say that this normal and healthy discontent can be channeled into the creative outlet of nonviolent direct action. And now this approach is being termed extremist.

But though I was initially disappointed at being categorized as an extremist, as I continued to think about the matter I gradually gained a measure of satisfaction from the label. Was not Jesus an extremist for love: "Love your enemies, bless them that curse you, do good to them that hate you, and pray for them which despitefully use you, and persecute you." Was not Amos an extremist for justice: "Let justice roll down like waters and righteousness like an ever-flowing stream." Was not Paul an extremist for the Christian gospel: "I bear in my body the marks of the Lord Jesus." Was not Martin Luther an extremist: "Here I stand; I cannot do otherwise, so help me God." And John Bunyan: "I will stay in jail to the end of my days before I make a butchery of my conscience." And Abraham Lincoln: "This nation cannot survive half slave and half free." And Thomas Jefferson: "We hold these truths to be self-evident, that all men are created equal. . . ." So the question is not whether we will be extremists, but what kind of extremists we will be. Will we be extremists for hate or for love? Will we be extremists for the preservation of injustice or for the extension of justice? In that dramatic scene on Calvary's hill three men were crucified. We must never forget that all three were crucified for the same crime—the crime of extremism. Two were extremists for immorality, and thus fell below their environment. The other, Jesus Christ, was an extremist for love, truth, and goodness, and thereby rose above his environment. Perhaps the South, the nation, and the world are in dire need of creative extremists.

I had hoped that the white moderate would see this need. Perhaps I was too optimistic; perhaps I expected too much. I suppose I should have realized that few members of the oppressor race can understand the deep groans and passionate yearnings of the oppressed race, and still fewer have the vision to see that injustice must be rooted out by strong, persistent, and determined action. I am thankful, however, that some of our white brothers in the South have grasped the meaning of this social revolution and committed themselves to it. They are still all too few in quantity, but they are big in quality. Some—such as Ralph McGill,

Lillian Smith, Harry Golden, James McBridge Dabbs, Ann Braden, and Sarah Patton Boyle—have written about our struggle in eloquent and prophetic terms. Others have marched with us down nameless streets of the South. They have languished in filthy, roach-infested jails, suffering the abuse and brutality of policemen who view them as "dirty nigger-lovers." Unlike so many of their moderate brothers and sisters, they have recognized the urgency of the moment and sensed the need for powerful "action" antidotes to combat the disease of segregation.

Let me take note of my other major disappointment. I have been so greatly disappointed with the white church and its leadership. Of course, there are some notable exceptions. I am not unmindful of the fact that each of you has taken some significant stands on this issue. I commend you, Reverend Stallings, for your Christian stand on this past Sunday, in welcoming Negroes to your worship service on a nonsegregated basis. I commend the Catholic leaders of this state for integrating Spring Hill College several years ago.

But despite these notable exceptions, I must honestly reiterate that I have been disappointed with the church. I do not say this as one of those negative critics who can always find something wrong with the church. I say this as a minister of the gospel, who loves the church; who was nurtured in its bosom; who has been sustained by its spiritual blessings and who will remain true to it as long as the cord of life shall lengthen.

When I was suddenly catapulted into the leadership of the bus protest 35 in Montgomery, Alabama, a few years ago, I felt we would be supported by the white church. I felt that the white ministers, priests, and rabbis of the South would be among our strongest allies. Instead, some have been outright opponents, refusing to understand the freedom movement and misrepresenting its leaders; all too many others have been more cautious than courageous and have remained silent behind the anesthetizing security of stained-glass windows.

In spite of my shattered dreams, I came to Birmingham with the hope that the white religious leadership of this community would see the justice of our cause and, with deep moral concern, would serve as the channel through which our just grievances could reach the power structure. I had hoped that each of you would understand. But again I have been disappointed.

I have heard numerous southern religious leaders admonish their worshipers to comply with a desegregation decision because it is the law, but I have longed to hear white ministers declare: "Follow this decree because integration is morally right and because the Negro is your brother." In the midst of blatant injustices inflicted upon the Negro, I have watched white churchmen stand on the sideline and mouth pious irrelevancies and sanctimonious trivialities. In the midst of a mighty struggle to rid our nation of racial and economic injustice, I have heard many ministers say: "Those are social issues, with which the gospel has no real concern." And I have watched many churches commit themselves to a completely otherworldly religion which makes a strange, un-Biblical distinction between body and soul, between the sacred and the secular.

I have traveled the length and breadth of Alabama, Mississippi, and all the other southern states. On sweltering summer days and crisp autumn mornings I have looked at the South's beautiful churches with their lofty spires pointing heavenward. I have beheld the impressive outlines of her massive religious-education buildings. Over and over I have found myself asking: "What kind of people worship here? Who is their God? Where were their voices when the lips of Governor Barnett dripped with words of interposition and nullification? Where were they when Governor Wallace gave a clarion call for defiance and hatred? Where were their voices of support when bruised and weary Negro men and women decided to rise from the dark dungeons of complacency to the bright hills of creative protest?"

Yes, these questions are still in my mind. In deep disappointment I have wept over the laxity of the church. But be assured that my tears have been tears of love. There can be no deep disappointment where there is not deep love. Yes, I love the church. How could I do otherwise? I am in the rather unique position of being the son, the grandson, and the great-grandson of preachers. Yes, I see the church as the body of Christ. But, oh! How we have blemished and scarred that body through social neglect and through fear of being nonconformists.

There was a time when the church was very powerful—in the time 40 when the early Christians rejoiced at being deemed worthy to suffer for what they believed. In those days the church was not merely a thermometer that recorded the ideas and principles of popular opinion; it was a thermostat that transformed the mores of society. Whenever the early Christians entered a town, the people in power became disturbed and immediately sought to convict the Christians for being "disturbers of the peace" and "outside agitators." But the Christians pressed on, in the conviction that they were "a colony of heaven," called to obey God rather than man. Small in number, they were big in commitment. They were too God-intoxicated to be "astronomically intimidated." By their effort and example they brought an end to such ancient evils as infanticide and gladiatorial contests.

Things are different now. So often the contemporary church is a weak, ineffectual voice with an uncertain sound. So often it is an archdefender of the status quo. Far from being disturbed by the presence of the church, the power structure of the average community is consoled by the church's silent—and often even vocal—sanction of things as they are.

But the judgment of God is upon the church as never before. If today's church does not recapture the sacrificial spirit of the early church, it will lose its authenticity, forfeit the loyalty of millions, and be dismissed as an irrelevant social club with no meaning for the twentieth century. Every day I meet young people whose disappointment with the church has turned into outright disgust.

Perhaps I have once again been too optimistic. Is organized religion too inextricably bound to the status quo to save our nation and the world? Perhaps I must turn my faith to the inner spiritual church, the church within the church, as the true *ekklesia* and the hope of the world. But again I am thankful to God that some noble souls from the ranks of organized religion have broken loose from the paralyzing chains of conformity and joined us as active partners in the struggle for freedom. They have left their secure congregations and walked the streets of Albany, Georgia, with us. They have gone down the highways of the South on tortuous rides for freedom. Yes, they have gone to jail with us. Some have been dismissed from their churches, have lost the support of their bishops and fellow ministers. But they have acted in the faith that right defeated is stronger than evil triumphant. Their witness has been the spiritual salt that has preserved the true meaning of the gospel in these troubled times. They have carved a tunnel of hope through the dark mountain of disappointment.

I hope the church as a whole will meet the challenge of this decisive hour. But even if the church does not come to the aid of justice, I have no despair about the future. I have no fear about the outcome of our struggle in Birmingham, even if our motives are at present misunderstood. We will reach the goal of freedom in Birmingham and all over the nation, because the goal of America is freedom. Abused and scorned though we may be, our destiny is tied up with America's destiny. Before the pilgrims landed at Plymouth, we were here. Before the pen of Jefferson etched the majestic words of the Declaration of Independence across the pages of history, we were here. For more than two centuries our forebears labored in this country without wages: they made cotton king; they built the homes of their masters while suffering gross injustice and shameful humiliation—and yet out of a bottomless vitality they continued to thrive and develop. If the inexpressible cruelties of slavery could not stop us, the opposition we now face will surely fail. We will win our freedom because the sacred heritage of our nation and the eternal will of God are embodied in our echoing demands.

Before closing I feel impelled to mention one other point in your statement that has troubled me profoundly. You warmly commended the 45

Birmingham police force for keeping "order" and "preventing violence." I doubt that you would have so warmly commended the police force if you had seen its dogs sinking their teeth into unarmed, nonviolent Negroes. I doubt that you would so quickly commend the policemen if you were to observe their ugly and inhumane treatment of Negroes here in the city jail; if you were to watch them push and curse old Negro women and young Negro girls; if you were to see them slap and kick old Negro men and young boys; if you were to observe them, as they did on two occasions, refuse to give us food because we wanted to sing our grace together. I cannot join you in your praise of the Birmingham police department.

It is true that the police have exercised a degree of discipline in handling the demonstrators. In this sense they have conducted themselves rather "nonviolently" in public. But for what purpose? To preserve the evil system of segregation. Over the past few years I have consistently preached that nonviolence demands that the means we use must be as pure as the ends we seek. I have tried to make clear that it is wrong to use immoral means to attain moral ends. But now I must affirm that it is just as wrong, or perhaps even more so, to use moral means to preserve immoral ends. Perhaps Mr. Connor and his policemen have been rather nonviolent in public, as was Chief Pritchett in Albany, Georgia, but they have used the moral means of nonviolence to maintain the immoral end of racial injustice. As T. S. Eliot has said. "The last temptation is the greatest treason: To do the right deed for the wrong reason."

I wish you had commended the Negro sit-inners and demonstrators of Birmingham for their sublime courage, their willingness to suffer, and their amazing discipline in the midst of great provocation. One day the South will recognize its real heroes. They will be the James Merediths, with the noble sense of purpose that enables them to face jeering and hostile mobs, and with the agonizing loneliness that characterizes the life of the pioneer. They will be old, oppressed, battered Negro women, symbolized in a seventy-two-year-old woman in Montgomery, Alabama, who rose up with a sense of dignity and with her people decided not to ride segregated buses, and who responded with ungrammatical profundity to one who inquired about her weariness: "My feets is tired, but my soul is at rest." They will be the young high school and college students, the young ministers of the gospel and a host of their elders, courageously and nonviolently sitting in at lunch counters and willingly going to jail for conscience' sake. One day the South will know that when these disinherited children of God sat down at lunch counters, they were in reality standing up for what is best in the American dream and for the most sacred values in our Judaeo-Christian heritage, thereby bringing our nation back to those great wells of democracy which were dug deep by the founding fathers in their formulation of the Constitution and the Declaration of Independence.

Never before have I written so long a letter. I'm afraid it is much too long to take your precious time. I can assure you that it would have been much shorter if I had been writing from a comfortable desk, but what else can one do when he is alone in a narrow jail cell, other than write long letters, think long thoughts, and pray long prayers?

If I have said anything in this letter that overstates the truth and indicates an unreasonable impatience, I beg you to forgive me. If I have said anything that understates the truth and indicates my having a patience that allows me to settle for anything less than brotherhood, I beg God to forgive me.

I hope this letter finds you strong in the faith. I also hope that circum- 50 stances will soon make it possible for me to meet each of you, not as an integrationist or a civil-rights leader but as a fellow clergyman and a Christian brother. Let us all hope that the dark clouds of racial prejudice will soon pass away and the deep fog of misunderstanding will be lifted from our fear-drenched communities, and in some not too distant to-morrow the radiant stars of love and brotherhood will shine over our great nation with all their scintillating beauty.

Yours for the cause of Peace and Brotherhood,
MARTIN LUTHER KING JR.

[1963]

KRISTIN RANDLETT

Confronting Cyberbullying

Kristin Randlett is a stay at home mom of three children. She is pursuing a degree in Radiologic Technology and plans to further her education, eventually completing a degree to become a Nuclear Medicine Technologist.

Eight days after Audrie Potts was assaulted by three high school boys at a party, she hanged herself. The boys had taken pictures of the assault, posted one on the internet, and passed other pictures around her high school. Not only the assault but also the cyberbullying were too much for Audrey Potts to endure (Paulson). Cyberbullying, according to the Colorado state bullying law, is defined as, "Any written or verbal expression or physical or electronic act or gesture intended to coerce, intimidate or cause any physical or mental or emotional harm to any student" (qtd. in McGraw). With incidences of cyberbullying on the rise and the safety and security of the students in jeopardy, school administrators must take a more firm stand against such acts. Cyberbullying should be a punishable offense in K-12 schools in the United States.

The increased presence of technology both at home and in the classroom/school has made cyberbullying more accessible. Cyberbullying differs from traditional bullying in that it creates a feeling of anonymity and decreases the uncomfortable sentiments associated with a face-to-face confrontation. Although traditional methods of bullying are seemingly less apparent, they are being carried out through social media outlets, such as Facebook, MySpace and Instagram. Bullies have the freedom to create false profiles and post pictures or derogatory comments about their victims without the threat of immediate disciplinary actions. It is true that parents/guardians should be responsible for the monitoring of their children's behavior on the internet; however, children and teens can operate the internet from sources parents may not have access to, or knowledge of. Carol McGraw in *The Colorado Springs Gazette* emphasized the extent of this issue: "While online and social media bullying often occurs at home or on mobile devices outside school, the resulting problems usually spill onto campuses." This overflow can be in the form of verbal confrontations, gossiping, name calling or even physical altercations. Safety in our schools should be the number one goal of our administrators and any threat to the safety of their students should be taken seriously.

Cyberbullying can cause depression and anxiety and, in extreme situations, result in suicide. According to an article in the *Pittsburg Post-Gazette*, "Bully victims have higher incidences of depression and anxiety that follow them throughout their lives" (Niederberger). There have been several occurrences where victims of cyberbullying have taken their own lives, largely as a result of the individuals feeling isolated and ostracized. Often times, students are afraid to report incidents of cyberbullying, fearing greater retaliation, or have reported them with little-to-no intervention from school administrators or law enforcement officials. Permanent damage can be done to both the victim and the bully.

Cyberbullying is preventable with stricter regulations and the implementation of consequences by school administrators. Several school districts have included sections in their student conduct handbooks regarding appropriate internet usage. "District 11 [in Colorado Springs] has an 'acceptable use' clause that governs school equipment. School policy is expansive, defining the school environment as: 'any non-district property or location where the behavior has a direct impact on school discipline or is detrimental to welfare and safety of students and staff'" (McGraw). Laws are still being developed and amended to protect the rights of both the students and the school administrators when it comes to implementing disciplinary actions. "They [some school districts] have been sued for exceeding authority and violating students' free speech rights" (McGraw). As a result, school administrators have had to use their own judgment in deciding whether or not to pursue disciplinary actions, often times, utilizing methods of "...peer mediation, counseling, [and] suspension" (McGraw) and in extreme cases of cyberbullying, contacting law enforcement officials.

Mary Niederberger states, "Cyberbullying is not increasing the number of bully cases... [but] it is a tool that can make the experience far more intense by allowing the bully to reach larger audiences." Cyberbullying, if left unaddressed, is a serious threat to the safety and well-being of the students the school administrators have a responsibility to protect. Students who are cyberbullied are subject to emotional, social, and physical harm. These repercussions can follow them throughout their lives, into adulthood, or in extreme situations result in suicide. School administrators must take a firm stand against such acts and safeguard the students from harm.

Works Cited

McGraw, Carol. "Cyberbullying Spills into Classrooms, Devastates Lives." *Gazette, The (Colorado Springs, CO)* 10 Feb. 2013: n.pag. *Newspaper Source*. Web. 25 Feb. 2013.

Niederberger, Mary. "Teacher Shares Bullying Expertise." *Pittsburgh Post-Gazette (PA)* 18 Nov. 2010: n.pag. *Newspaper Source*. Web. 25 Feb. 2013.

Paulson, Amanda. "Audrie Pott Family to Sue Teens and Their Families for 'Wrongful Death'." *Christian Science Monitor* 15 Apr. 2013: n.pag. *Newspaper Source*. Web. 12 June 2013.

BONNIE HOLLINGSWORTH

Home-Schooling: A Good Alternative to Public School

Bonnie Hollingsworth enrolled in Pueblo Community College after she was homeschooled as a child and a teen. She currently plans to earn a degree in nursing and work in a variety of settings.

The National Center for Education Statistics reports that the number of people who home-school grew about seventy four percent from 1999 to 2007 (United States, "Fast Facts"). Home-school is not for everyone, but to some parents it is their best alternative to public schooling. Because my parents home-schooled me ever since I was school age, I learned the benefits of home-schooling. Although some say home-schooling will interfere with the child's social development, home-school should be considered for children because they may learn better, have fewer negative peer influences, and be safer.

Home-schooled children may learn better because the student will have more attention from the teacher, more time to ask questions, and more styles in which to learn. On the other hand, in public schools the teacher has many different students, so he/she cannot give each student the time and attention that one might need to learn well. According to Michael Romanowski, a professor at the Center for Teacher Education in Ohio, children who are home-schooled usually test at or even higher than the national average in standardized tests (128). Public school teachers have many different students in a class which makes it hard to adapt to each child's needs. In home-schooling, however, there could be one teacher to maybe one to three students. The teacher can then focus on each student's learning style, whether it be tactile, auditory, or visual, whereas some public schools have a curriculum which they follow. According to Bonnie Mackey, Kasha Reese, and Wade Mackey, the authors of the article "Demographics of Home Schoolers:...," nearly forty-five percent of home-schooled children receive college degrees while only about thirty-seven percent of non-home-schooled children receive a college degree. Furthermore, home-schooled children have better grade point averages while in college. According to Michael Cogan, who wrote an article in the *Journal of College Admission*, in one year of college the average home-schooler's GPA was 3.41, while the GPA of students who went to public school was only 3.12. In a four year college, home-schooled students still have a better GPA. Home-schooled children have an average of 3.46 GPA while public school graduates had 3.16 GPA.

Moreover, some parents home-school their children because they are worried about the influences of other children. Some public schools have been known to have drugs on the premises. According to The National Center for Education Statistics, in the year 2004, 1.4 million crimes were committed on school campuses; in 2005 a fourth of high school students let it be known that they had access to or had purchased illegal drugs in the last year from other students while on the school premises. Parents might not know that their child is smoking or doing drugs until the child is addicted. Parents may never find out what their children have done, said, or the way they acted that day at school. It makes the parents wonder whom their children are associating with, and many parents are afraid it is with the ones who will get their children involved in drugs.

Furthermore, home school is safer for children. According to The National Center for Education Statistics, in 2005 an average of fifty-eight percent of students said that they have been bullied about one to two times during the last six months, while eight percent said on average during that time period they were bullied almost every day (United States, "Indicators"). On many school campuses there are fights, bullying incidents, and weapons that can cause much harm. Children would be safer in an environment where parents can watch them and make sure none of these situations will happen. From July 2004 to June 2005, children age five to eighteen were victims of twenty-one homicides and seven suicides that happened while the children were at school. Also NCES relates that in 2004, 107,000 young students between ages twelve and eighteen were victimized with severe crimes such as "rape, sexual assault, robbery, and aggravated assault" (United States, "Indicators").

Conversely, one of the many arguments people have against home-schooling is that children will suffer from a lack of social life. However, home-schooled children have more contact with different age groups and backgrounds than themselves, whereas public school children have limitations to classrooms that consist of about thirty-five other students who are about the same age and possibly have the same background as themselves (Romanowski 126). I was personally home-schooled all my life. In high school I volunteered at Parkview Medical Center, which taught me how to interact with several people, not just the ones my own age. Parents of home-schooled children need to make sure their children are involved in field trips with other children, a sports group, or even in volunteering. Furthermore, there are many programs for home-schooled children so they can talk and interact. For example, according to Beth Jokinen, who wrote an article in *The Lima News*, a local school called Pioneer Academy welcomes home-school children one day a week. Students can then participate in classes "such as music, band, physical education and Spanish." There are also schools which allow home-schooled children to participate in school sports. Richard Locker, a journalist for *The Commercial Appeal*, wrote that home-schooled children now have the chance to try out for public school sports teams just like the other children who are attending that public school.

Another reason parents might not want to home-school is that children will not be adequately equipped for real world situations because they were too sheltered. Nevertheless, there was a survey done in 1991 on people who were home-schooled. The survey showed that none of the home-schooled children were welfare recipients or unemployed, nearly sixty-six percent were self-employed, and about ninety-four percent agreed that through their home-school experience they learned to be more independent (Romanowski 127). In the same article, Romanowski writes that children who were home-schooled participated in the community more than the average American adult. He went on to say that nearly seventy-one percent participated in community service while only about thirty-seven percent of non-home schooled children participated. People who were home-schooled are more likely to donate money to political causes and help the person running for office by working for him/her. Home-schooled children also show a better work ethic and stronger values and morals which show in their college success (128).

Even though some people are worried about home-schooling their children, home-schooling is a good alternative to public school. The growth rate alone will show that more and more Americans have come to that same conclusion. Parents need to consider the option of home-schooling their children before they place their children in public school because children might learn better, have fewer negative peer influences, and be safer, and it would allow the children to become good citizens who interact well with others. I was home-schooled, and even though home school is most definitely not perfect, I am glad today that I was.

Works Cited

Cogan, Michael F. "Exploring Academic Outcomes of Homeschooled Students." *Journal of College Admission* 208 (2010) n. pag.: *Academic Search Premier*. Web. 11 Apr. 2013.

Jokinen, Beth L. "Temple Creates Enrichment Program for Home-School Families." *Lima News, The* (OH) (2012): n. pag. *Newspaper Source*. Web. 11 Apr. 2013.

Locker, Richard. "Unanimous: Bill Allowing Home School Students to Play Public School Sports Passes Tennessee Senate." *Commercial Appeal, The (Memphis TN)* (2013): n. pag. *Newspaper Source*. Web. 11 Apr. 2013.

Macky, Bonnie W., Kasha Rees, and Wade C. Mackey. "Demographics of Home Schoolers: A Regional Analysis within the National Parameters." *Education 132.1* (2011): n. pag. *Academic Search Premier*. Web. 27 Mar. 2013.

Romanowski, Michael. "Revisiting the Common Myths about Home Schooling." *Clearing House: A Journal of Educational Strategies, Issues and Ideas* 79.3 (2006): 125-129. Web. 16 Apr. 2013.

United States. Dept. of Education. U.S National Center for Education Statistics. "Fast Facts." The National Center for Education Statistics. Web. 3 Apr. 2013.

---.---. ---. "Indicators of School Crime and Safety: 2006." The National Center for Education Statistics. Web. 3 Apr. 2013.

JOSLYNE LOVELACE

Benefits of Early College

Joslyne Lovelace, an early college student at Pueblo Community College, graduated in 2010 with a high school degree and an associate's degree. She plans to attend Colorado State University at Fort Collins and pursue a career in biomedical engineering.

Many American families sit around the dinner table, discussing how to send their children to college and wondering if they will ever have the money. The cost of college does not stop at tuition; there are also books, room and board, food, and many other expenses. The cost of college continues to rise. Because of tight state and federal budgets, students have to pay more of their college costs from their own pocketbooks (Kelley). Although students can apply for loans, they will spend years paying those loans off. Whatever the cost, however, college is one of the keys to being a successful adult. Therefore, more people should have the opportunity to attend. The early college program is the answer to many of these struggling families' prayers. Early college is a program in which high school students take college courses that count towards both high school and college credits. A portion of these high school students earn an associate's degree along with their high school diploma. Unfortunately, some people are concerned about the success of the program and the maturity of the high school students, but evidence indicates that early college is a rational option for parents and students.

Undeniably, college is expensive and difficult for many families to afford. Because of our state's economy, we are seeing many colleges and universities increasing student tuition and cost of services to meet their programs' needs. Fortunately, early college pays for the classes and the books. Some families cannot afford the ever-increasing cost of higher education and need the program desperately. A recent study indicates that many families in need do take advantage of early college; almost 60 percent of early college participants claim the need to reduce the cost of their children's education as one of their main reasons for their interest in this program. ("Overview"). These families are in need of the help to send their children to college. On average, a year of public college costs about five thousand dollars, which can strain the pocketbooks of many American families. On average a person with a high school diploma will most likely earn a salary of $23,829, compared to the salary of someone with a bachelor's degree, which is about $43,954. Those with college educations on average earn about twice as much money a year as those who stopped their education after high school ("How Will I"). Therefore, as much as young people can't afford to go to college in these difficult economic times, they almost can't afford not to go to college.

Although saving money is a major benefit of early college, one big issue among opponents of the early college program is the maturity level of the high school students. Granted, some high school students do not have the right attitude for college, but this is not true for all high school students. The program is a choice made by the students and their parents, and the families are only putting themselves at risk when enrolling a teenager who cannot handle college. Similar to traditional college students, early college students are tested to ensure proper placement into courses; in addition, they are interviewed by counselors as a way to assess their maturity level. But unlike traditional students, if early college students fail their courses, then they are required to pay for the classes—a policy that motivates parental involvement in the children's education. As a result of these requirements, most of the early college students have proven that they are mature enough to handle college courses. Still, skeptics claim that too many early college students "ditch" their classes, but recent studies show that the average attendance rate for early college students is over 90 percent ("Overview"). Not only are early college students mature enough to be in a college environment, but the students' level of maturity and sense of responsibility continue to grow through the program—interacting with adults and facing real life situations. With college courses come more responsibilities for the students; being able to take on all the challenges of college will better prepare teens for the future.

Another reason that early college is a good choice is that some high school students are not comfortable in the high school environment and would rather surround themselves with a more adult crowd. Many high school students do not take school seriously and take time away from the students who want to learn. However, in college most of the students are more motivated and therefore want to learn and do well. Because of the motivation of the college students, classroom discussions are interesting and engaging. I used to dread going to high school. I would drag myself out of bed in the morning, moaning, and would beg my mom to let me stay home since I didn't see the value of being in the classroom. Now, in the early college program, the classroom experience is meaningful and exciting. As a result, I love school. The days do not drag on forever as they did in the past, and I actually look forward to my classes. My attitude about school has gone from completely negative to positive.

Because of my new found motivation, I have also learned more and go home with my brain filled with new knowledge. There are many adults in my classes, and I know that they are much wiser and more intelligent than I. When I go to class, I learn not only from my teachers but also from my classmates.

However, critics of the program argue that the high school students are taking up space in the classroom that should be reserved for paying students; critics insist that the early college program is taking away from the college students and the college. However, high school students in the program are not the only ones who receive a college education without personally paying for the courses. Some receive scholarships, yet they take up a place in the classroom. Although I do not pay the bills, the school is still given the same amount of tuition money as any other student. At my school, Southern Colorado Academy, there is no staff for grades eleven and twelve. Instead, the students attend Pueblo Community College. Because my high school doesn't have those extra staff members, there is extra money to use for early college tuition money. The fact that the program is free for the participating students does not mean that it is free from tuition completely. The colleges still get the same amount of money for every student. Also, Pueblo Community College receives funding for the number of students enrolled, including high school students. Thus, having high school students attend colleges such as Pueblo Community College benefits the colleges financially, enhancing the learning environment of other college students by funding and increasing support services. In sum, early college does not take away from other students but actually helps all students succeed in and enrich their education.

Finally, opponents of early college question the success of this program. However, the Early College High School Initiative, funded by The Bill & Melinda Gates Foundation, along with Carnegie Corporation of New York, the Ford Foundation, the W.K. Kellogg Foundation, and other local foundations, attests to the program's effectiveness and success. In 2007, the first graduating classes of three early college high schools were given diplomas, and of those 115 seniors, 80 percent were accepted into four-year colleges, 85 percent had 30 to 60 college credits before high school graduation, and over 57 percent graduated with an associate's degree ("Overview"). The statistics are very impressive and support the success of the early college program. The challenges that colleges place on all students motivate the high school student to perform at a high standard. Karen W. Arenson, a New York Times journalist, reports that "less accomplished students—including those in danger of dropping out—are capable of handling more difficult work, and ... more of them will graduate if they are challenged more." The rigor offered by colleges inspires high school students to succeed. It is likely that many students, had it not have been for the early college program, would not have gone to college. Some wouldn't have made it all the way through high school. The fact that more students are going to college and are excelling in their work speaks volumes for the early college program. Can the evidence be stronger than this?

The many advantages of the early college program make this option realistic for parents. Although the early college program has some flaws that need work, it is a program that I am honored to be a part of. Because of the early college program, I won't have to spend ten years paying off student loans. I get to be in a classroom where I feel comfortable and engaged, not an easy emotion for a teenager to achieve. With this program, I have been given more responsibilities and have been able to grow more. The early college program has better prepared me for the future, and I am so grateful that I have been given the opportunity to participate in it. The early college program is a dream come true for many people. It has definitely helped out my family financially and has reduced the stress of paying for college. At a time when our nation is so concerned about the next generation's education, the early college program should be supported by all as a way of enriching and raising the level and the success of high school students' education.

Works Cited

Arenson, Karen. "'Early College' Gains Ground In Education." *New York Times* 14 July 2003, sec 1:13. *Academic Search Premier.* Web. 3 Nov. 2008.

"How Will I Pay For College?" College is Too Expensive. N.p. 2007. Web. 27 Oct. 2008.

Kelley, Rob. "Average College Cost Breaks." CNNMoney.com. Cable News Network. 27 Oct. 2006. Web. 3 Nov. 2008.

"Overview & FAQ." The Early College High School Initiative. N.p. 2007. Web. 27 Oct. 2008.

DANIEL LYONS

Ban Antibacterial Products

Daniel Lyons owns and operates a janitorial service specializing in cleaning high tech communications buildings. He earned an Associate of Science degree and plans to transfer to CSU-Pueblo for a B.S. degree in microbiology.

Who among us has not been told to wash our hands? That is a phrase we all have heard numerous times during our lifetime. There are reminders posted in the washrooms of restaurants, colleges, gas stations and several other establishments. Television commercials portraying bacterial germs as mean and ugly organisms remind us that using only antibacterial agents can kill these germs effectively. However, some studies have shown regular hand washing with regular soap is as effective in killing germs without antibacterial chemicals. These same studies have found antibacterial chemicals in our sewage systems, farming land, and the waterways. The integration of these chemicals, with other widely used chemical agents like chlorine, found in most municipalities as a water sterilizer, have toxic influence on us and our environment. The disposal of these agents, namely triclocarbon and triclosan, has no oversight of any organization whatsoever. Consequently, our unregulated uses of these products are leading to organisms that are resistant to antibiotics that are much needed in our society to fight more serious forms of staphylococcal bacterial infections. Therefore, the manufacture and use of antibacterial agents should be banned.

Manufacturers of antibacterial products erroneously assert that we are all in danger from microbial invasions and should use their products to protect ourselves and that we need to do so with antibacterial agents. A recent finding by the Food and Drug Administration concludes there is no evidence that antibacterial products protect us any better than regular soaps and detergents. The most commonly used antibacterial agents, triclocarbon and triclosan, aren't just found in soaps and detergents; they are in deodorants, body washes, cosmetics, cleaning supplies, hand sanitizers, mouthwashes, and most unfortunately, toothpaste (Adams). Triclosan, the most widely used antibacterial agent, is found in several brands of toothpaste. This is alarming because triclosan reacts with chlorine, which is used by most municipalities as a water sterilizer and pumped to our faucets. As we brush our teeth, the triclosan and chlorine mix to form a chemical reaction resulting in chloroform. Chloroform is a known carcinogen. In essence, we are using our mouths as a mixing bowl. Even more alarming is the fact that the combination of triclosan and chlorine is "similar to the dioxins found in the compound Agent Orange" (Adams).

In addition, toothpaste makers argue that they use triclosan because it helps to reduce plaque and kill bacteria; however, triclosan does harm by causing gum damage. Triclosan is also marketed under the brand names of Microban and Biofresh, which are used as an additive in bedding, textiles, socks, toys, and different types of plastics used in the manufacture of cutting boards (Adams). Studies have shown these antibacterial agents are not needed to keep us safe and may have long term implications. According to Worldwatch Institute, a globally-focused environmental research organization, "In the United States, seventy-five percent of liquid soaps and thirty percent of bar soaps now contain triclosan and other germ-fighting compounds whose prevalence can foster the growth of bacterial resistance" (Adams).

Manufacturers claim their product is effective in killing bacteria. Triclosan and other widely used chemicals are indeed killing bacteria, even the bacteria we need for everyday sustenance. We have bacteria in our bodies to provide many important functions such as keeping our immune system operating smoothly, breaking down vitamins in our digestive system for use by other bodily systems, and controlling our serotonin levels to make us feel happy (Adler).

Antibacterial agents wind up in our wastewater from hand washing, dishwashing, and other methods of disposal. Should we care? Bacteria perform many actions to break down waste products in sewage systems by eating the waste and turning it into disposable forms to re-enter the natural purification processes. Without these beneficial bacteria, rural homeowners would be responsible for waste transport to a satisfactory disposal site. This disposal method would be unpleasant for obvious reasons and could possibly lead to illegal dumping in remote areas. Big cities have waste water treatment plants to process the waste, but the process does not do any type of antibacterial agent removal, so these agents just float along to wherever they wind up. Along the journey to their final resting place, the antibacterial agents interact chemically and biologically with hospital antibiotic waste, household antibacterial waste, pharmaceutical waste, and who knows what else. These agents start to react with other organisms and evolve into something else, something dreadful, and something deadly—antibiotic resistant germs (Ricks). As for the germs' final resting place, the majority of this toxic mix is spread onto expansive agricultural fields where we grow and harvest our food supply. The average American produces forty-seven pounds of solid waste sludge per year. This calculates into several billion pounds of sludge with sixty six percent of that sludge being dumped on our farms (Cone). The several cases of e-coli poisoned spinach last year might have been a result of this reckless method of disposal. Studies have not been thoroughly conducted yet on the amount of triclosan and triclocarbon residue that is consumed along with our food.

Finally, manufacturers mislead us into believing that these antibacterial products are safe. They base their claim on toxicological tests performed by placing high doses of their products directly on the skin with no apparent signs of harm. On the contrary, no one yet knows what long term exposure is doing to us in a very slow manner. What we do know is that the harm to us indirectly may cause uncontrollable widespread death for us all. According to Professor Kim Kushner, science faculty at Pueblo Community College, "the overuse of antibiotics and the misuse of antibacterial agents are leading us to a deadly, resistant form of bacterial 'superbug.' " Her statements seem prophetic, especially with the attention-grabbing headline of the Methicillin-resistant Staphylococcus aureus, or MRSA, which killed nineteen thousand people in the United States in 2005 (Adler).

Any organism, whether animal, human, or bacterial, has built in mechanisms to protect itself from intruders. These mechanisms come in contact with something foreign and produce antibodies to resist the action of the intruder. When the antibodies finally come into contact with the invader, whether to kill the organism or slightly alter the organism to coexist with it or just build up immunity to it, the guard is let down, and peace is at hand. The continuing cycle passes down the line, interacts with other organisms, and starts another chain reaction of invading and evolving with whatever the protectant is and passing down again to some other invader. This is a vicious cycle that our scientists are fighting on a daily basis. The numbers of mutations an organism can go through heavily outweigh what tools are available to our scientists to combat these mutations.

With no organization to control the use of antibacterial agents, the scary results will continue to be analyzed. We do need to practice good hygiene, but we do not need to use antibacterial agents to produce the desired results. Will we, as a nation, stop using these products on our own? With manufacturers reminding us often of the dangers of germs invading our lives and the diligence we must maintain to keep them under control, the possibility of self-restraint appears unlikely. The results of scientific research regarding the unregulated interaction of antibacterial agents with other chemical compounds, the destruction of much needed homeostatic bacteria, the uncontrolled disposal of waste sludge, and the resulting antibiotic resistance to certain germs indicate that we must ban the manufacture and use of antibacterial products.

Works Cited

Adams, Mike. "Toxic Chemical Triclosan Commonly Found in Antibacterial Soaps, Toothpaste Products". *NaturalNews.com*. The Natural News Network, 29 October 2007. Web. 2 December 2007.

Adler, Jerry, and Jeneen Interlandi. "Caution: Killing Germs May Be Hazardous to Your Health." *Newsweek*. 29 October 2007. Web. 2 December 2007.

Cone, Marla. "Threat Seen from Antibacterial Soap Chemicals". *Los Angeles Times*. Los Angeles Times, 10 May 2006. Web. 15 November 2007.

Kushner, Kim. Personal interview. 20 November 2007.

Ricks, Delthia. "Scientists Find Traces of Antibiotics in Waterways." *Newsday*. 29 October 2007: n. pag. *Newspaper Source*. Web. 15 November 2007.

JAMEY LIONETTE

Mass Production of Food
Is Ruining Our Health

Jamey Lionette is a food activist and consultant for developing local
and sustainable food systems in the United States and Canada. He
organized the 2010 Boston Local Food Festival and, until 2010, ran the
family-owned Lionette's Market and the Garden of Eden restaurant in
Boston, Massachusetts.

Lionette's essay "Mass Production of Food is Ruining Our Health"
encourages readers to stop shopping at chain grocery stores and con-
suming mass-produced food that promotes agro-business at the
expense of local farms and shops. He critiques the American consumer
mentality that demands "exotic" and out-of-season food—such as
tomatoes during the winter—year round at low cost. Lionette explains
that Americans don't understand the true cost of food, and he argues
that "local, clean, and sustainable food" should be a right not a
privilege.

I am not a scientist, journalist, or other specialist. I sell food. I help run a
family-owned and operated neighborhood market and café that buys
and sells predominantly local, clean, and sustainable food. I cannot
speak about the reality of our food supply around most of the world. I
can only can speak of what is happening in the first world, where, unfortunately, only the privileged elite can choose to put real food on their
dinner tables.

Lately it seems every mass media newspaper or magazine, from the
New York Times to *Rolling Stone*, has an article digging into the true filth
that most food in the U.S. really is. Some people are actually questioning
mass produced and monoculture organic food. Even *Time* magazine
proclaimed "Local Is the New Organic" on its cover. Everywhere I turn
people tell me that there is a new wind in the U.S.; that people are now
concerned about eating local, clean, and sustainable food. From my

Jamey Lionette, "Mass Production of Food Is Ruining Our Health." From *Manifestos
on the Future of Food & Seed*, Edited by Vandana Shiva (South End Press, 2007).
Reprinted by permission of the author.

vantage point in the market, behind the counter, I just don't see it. Yes, in Massachusetts there are more farms today than in the last 20 or so years, but fewer total acres than ever recorded. Farmers' markets are becoming popular or perhaps trendy. Chain supermarkets are "listening to their customers" and capitalizing on cheap "organic" food. But the chain-supermarket owners are some of the same people who screwed up our food supply in the first place. How can we trust them?

Outdoor food markets are a mainstay in most cultures in the world and were once a given in our culture. Now most people go there to shop for the luxury food treats (locally grown food) and get their staples at the supermarket. I think that because of the Depression (when there was no money to spend on food) and World War II (when there was rationing and everyone was focused on the war effort) Americans lost their taste-buds. Along came the mass-produced foods of the 1950s at cheap prices. Supermarkets were a "progressive" thing, as suburban living was progressive. Rural culture and production was frowned upon as old-fashioned and primitive. Food from all over the world suddenly became available and at prices lower than local food. Protecting America's foreign interest, the beginning of what we now call globalization, became a new form of colonialism. Foreign resources, raw materials as well as labor, were now easily exploitable by the nation's new superpower status. As the economy grew, money filtered down to the managerial and to some of the working class and was coupled with an influx of cheap products made cheaply and available to most classes of the U.S. Consumerism took off. Our food changed as well, especially with faster transport and technologies trickery to extend the shelf life of food. Seasonal produce became available year round; exotic food (such as bananas and oranges in Boston) became readily available and affordable. Everything was cheaper, the shopping was more convenient, and exotic foods became staples in our diet. Small and local farms shut down or were forced into monoculture farming. A disconnect sprouted between our diets and our food sources. An orange, once a special and rare treat, became an everyday commodity.

Supermarkets are part of mainstream America's identity. Working-class people have little choice but to shop at conventional supermarkets. Middle-class people can shop at places like Whole Foods and appease their consciences with the notion that that food is safer and tastier than conventional supermarket food. And those of the flat earth society— middle- and upper-class people who do not believe that their climate is changing, that a global market is a bad thing, or that our food systems are in trouble—favor the conventional supermarket. However, both conventional and progressive supermarkets operate on the same model: mass-produced foods, made cheaply, and sold at cheap prices.

Supermarkets sell commodities. They buy mass-produced food from 5
big business. This model of efficiency, which mirrored the production of
things like automobiles and VCRs, is what created the mess our food
supply is in. Efficient ordering and deliveries, no seasonal variety of
stock, little to no blemishes (whether natural or from human error), significant quantities—enough to keep all those shelves constantly filled
with whatever the customer might want. I describe this model as "I want
what I want when I want it," and it goes against everything about food
that is local, clean, and sustainable. It cannot be done at a mass level. . . .

People first bought cheap food because they either did not have enough
money or felt like they were beating the system by spending less than
they budgeted for food that week. Over time our budgets became based
on the price of cheap food, so that now, during the rare moment of seeing real food, the price tag appears exorbitant. Our wages and salaries,
our rent and utilities, all are tied to our cheaply priced food.

Many people who can actually afford local, clean, sustainable food
buy it only when it is trendy, sold at boutique shops, or for a special
occasion. Those from the class which struggles to afford mass-produced
food certainly cannot afford the real price of food in the U.S. One often-
overlooked agent of gentrification and, after rent increases, one of the
best ways to ruin a neighborhood is by shopping at chain supermarkets.
Local neighborhood markets close or survive by becoming convenience
stores. Farmers' markets become a trendy place to buy a few novelty
items: "Oooh look at this peach. I bought it from a farmer!" Once the
small markets are gone, only supermarkets are left. We are so out of
touch with the struggle to get food, because of how much cheap food is
available in the country, that we do not see a pattern of destruction.

The more we buy mass-produced foods, the more it empowers agro-
business and the fewer farms there will be. The more we shop at supermarkets, the fewer neighborhood markets there will be. Already we are
almost trapped by agro-business and its sales outlets. Soon, there will be
no escape. As it stands right now, only a privileged few can afford real,
clean, and sustainable food; soon, even the privileged will have little
access to such food. The fewer local farms we have, the more expensive
their food becomes and the more difficult it is for local farms to feed the
local population. Once the farms are gone, only mass-produced food is
left.

Hadley, Massachusetts, is known as having the best asparagus in the
world. Though just an hour or so outside of Boston, it is near impossible
to find asparagus grown in Hadley in Boston. Futures of the asparagus are
sold; mostly to France and Japan, I am told. Instead of a wonderful spring
vegetable for a local dish, Hadley asparagus has become a boutique item

for other parts of the world. Yet in spring, summer, winter, or fall, asparagus flown in from Peru is half the price of in-season asparagus grown on a family farm in New England. And I must admit it seems a bit shameful to complain about such a situation in the U.S., when so many peoples around the world local resources have been diverted to produce food for Americans.

The late summer is tomato season in New England. The glory of a local tomato salad on a warm summer night in Boston is something which we can only enjoy a couple of months a year. The flavor of our farmers' tomatoes are spectacular. Especially when bought at a local shop or farmers' market, where we actually speak with the people involved in harvesting and distributing our food, people who are part of our community. These tomatoes were not sprayed with anything; the soil was not ruined by chemicals or monoculture farming. These tomatoes traveled only a few dozen miles and were grown outside, thus using only a little energy and creating little pollution. The farmer, part of our community, was deservedly paid and did not exploit anyone or the land. No one was ripped off during the whole transaction, and the tomatoes were available to everyone in Boston during the late summer months.

Yet the rest of the year we still expect to have fresh tomatoes available, and they are called for in many dishes. Fresh tomatoes are considered year-round staples. There is never any questioning tomatoes in March, their integrity or their source. We have become used to hydroponic tomatoes flown in from Mexico or Holland. Instead of focusing our efforts on bringing in tomatoes year-round to Boston, we should focus making the Northeast corridor able to feed itself now and in the future. At the very least, these factory-grown tomatoes do make our local tomatoes taste even more wonderful. We are so used to the mealy, flavorless (or artificially flavored) hydro-tomato that when we taste a real one, it seems so special. This is one reason why local farmers are not perceived as the people who raise our food, but as the producers of specialty items.

Another reason farmers are considered purveyors of specialty foods is their prices. Let us end the idea right now that local, clean, and sustainable foods result in a high profit for the producer and the retailer—trust me, there is absolutely no money in sustainable food. When food is handled as sustenance—not as a commodity—there is little profit to be had. That is why real food is so rare and so hard to come by now. The perverted twist is that it would seem logical that food transported for days around the world would cost more than something fresh and local. But quite the opposite is true. Nobody considers what the true price of real food is. Nobody is outraged that what most working-class people can afford, and even the middle class can afford, is nothing more than mass-produced, cheapened food.

There are, of course, the Whole Foods, Wal-Marts, Trader Joes, and other chain supermarkets trying to sell organic foods. Everyone knows these places are cheaper than local markets and farmers' markets, but rarely do people think about how supermarkets work. People are generally aware of the smaller mark-up chain supermarkets can afford, as compared with an independent neighborhood market, as well as all the corporate capital and funding behind them. But few often think about what is involved in producing enough of a particular food for every shelf of their hundreds or thousands of outlets across the region or country. You can't see the devastating effects of monoculture farming in the sterile and lifeless supermarket. The food looks so perfect and seems so abundant. And with such cheap prices, why ask questions? Sustainable farming does not have the ability to be mass produced; it cannot be sold at the level of a chain supermarkets. Corners must be cut to keep costs low, production must increase to fill the shelves, the laws of nature must be beaten by science to allow for year round production, and if the weather cannot yet be defeated, then the product should be mass-produced and imported from another part of the world.

Listen, Thanksgiving 2006: Whole Foods Boston was selling a "fully pastured naturally raised" turkey for $1.99/lb. That is painfully cheap. Was it trying to compete with the half-dozen small town turkey farmers still left in Massachusetts or the handful of farmers selling turkeys to their regular customers at the farmers' markets or through community-supported agriculture (CSA)? Probably not. Such consumers of locally raised food still have an appreciation for the tradition of buying a turkey from the same place every year or still get pleasure from buying their turkeys directly from their friend, the farmer, or a neighborhood shop. Whole Foods was trying to compete with the other big supermarkets, who sell cheap food.

Whole Foods (and the supermarkets imitating it) will be the death of 15 the movement for clean, local, and fair food for many reasons, but this is an important one. By dropping the price so low, and using claims and slogans designed not by farmers but by slick salespeople, it has set the expectation that clean food can be as cheap as, or just slightly more expensive than, filthy food. Many people could afford to make the jump from Butterball to a Whole Food bird and, with that jump, assume that the bird was safer, more sustainable, and cleaner. So now any farmer charging a real price is seen as greedy or overpriced. Like Wal-Mart's cheap organic, Whole Foods has cheapened (in integrity, as well as price) naturally raised meats and clean food. It lowers the bar by allowing cheap mass-production and corner-cutting, all to sell cheap food that you think is something it is not. There is tokenistic buying of local food and various labels to suggest a certain quality to the consumer. Because we have so few local farms left, it is easy for a chain supermarket to buy some local food and appear to be supportive of local farms. For most people, this is the easy and convenient way to feel as though they are doing the right thing. But it was the supermarket in the first place that helped reduce the number of farms and transformed our understanding of what local farms are.

Organic food is by no means synonymous with clean food. What should we expect, considering a food supply which is mass-produced will be shipped all over the world? And how did the E. coli get into the spinach? Nobody knows. The apparatus is too big. We are concerned, but we are overwhelmed and more importantly completely removed from our food; we have no idea how to eat locally. I am sure nearly half of Boston goes months without ever eating a single bite of local food.

Are people buying store-brand organics duped or misled? Not exactly. The argument for mass-produced organic food is that at least it is a lesser of two evils. I would agree that mass-produced organic or mass-produced naturally raised is not as bad as mass-produced conventional food, but it is still bad. Are we content with eating bad food? Where is the outrage at choosing between bad and worse? Within the first world, on a day-to-day basis, there is barely a struggle to obtain food. But obtaining clean food is a struggle. And to complicate matters are savvy marketing and confusing legal and nonlegal claims. Do the research on what the USDA allows for the claim "free-range" or "organic." They are by no means what you would expect. To be labeled free-range, the law states only that once a bird is old enough to safely venture outside (fair enough, small chicks are at risk outside to predators, weather, diseases, etc.) that they can be kept inside as long as they have access to the outdoors. Often this means a small hole in the wall leading to a small, lifeless patch of land, which the bird never bothers going out to. And for organic—just a few hours outdoors (not necessarily free of a cage) and nothing but USDA certified organic feed. Great, but that feed may not be what that animal wants to eat at all. Mass-produced food and monoculture farming does nothing good for the land. It burns it up. It is not sustainable. Organic or conventional—if it is produced in favor of profit over sustainability it cannot last forever. . . .

This is our society. A society that has no interest in banning feedlots or the excessive/exclusive feeding of grains, hormones, animal by-products, and antibiotics to cows and seemingly covers up any connection with these practices to E. coli. Worse, our health officials and beef industry leaders come up with a chemical injection to kill possible E. coli and dabble in using pro-biotic injections to make our food "safe." What did you expect? These are the same people who actually believed that forcing cows to be cannibals in confined quarters—which gave us mad-cow disease—for the sake of cheap beef and high profits was not a bad idea. If you could witness how most of our food is produced, you would not eat it; you would be outraged. We are so far removed from our food.

People think that by washing the vegetable with water that all the chemicals are washed off. Even more absurd, many of these same people will buy bottled water because they don't trust the tap water to drink (but they think it is clean enough to rinse their food with?). People don't worry about chemicals possibly absorbed into the food and seeping into the land. People choose shiny fruit covered in wax and pesticide over the uglier, misshapen, dull-colored clean fruit from a farm because they believe it will taste better or is safer. How ludicrous is it when mass-produced food is just called "tomato" or "beef," but real food must be called "NOFA Certified Organic-locally grown on a small, clean, sustainable farm, free of all pesticides heirloom tomato" or "100 percent grass-fed/grass finished, hormone-free, antibiotic-free, animal-by-product-free, fully pastured, naturally raised on a small, local, sustainable family-farm beef." This is a society that has organic corn syrup! There is fair reason to be disgusted and outraged at our current food supply and culture of convenience that has created and perpetuated this mess.

It is nice to believe that eating is a revolutionary act, but sooner or 20 later someone is going to have to call this system out. When a few people start ruining our food, we must take action against those people. When a system has failed, we must change that system. When we are perpetuating that system because of our laziness and lust for convenience, then we must change, or else we will collapse. I cannot think of any point in history when a food supply has been so dangerous. Food's place in our culture and community has faded into cheap traditions. Our planet's fertile land has decayed, been poisoned, and been transformed into factories while we have been too busy and out of touch with our food to notice. The people who know how to use the land to produce food have lost their place on the land, and we did not notice because we no longer know who produces our food. Our food supply is being linked to long-term damage such as heart disease and cancer. And now our food is killing us instantly. Not a week passes it seems that there is not some kind of deadly outbreak. What are you doing about it? We can easily envision a society based on sustainable food; most cultures throughout history have had sustainable farming practices. Basically, Grandma had it right and the progressive supermarkets had it all wrong. We do not necessarily have to turn back the clock and return to an agrarian society, but let's understand what Grandma was doing and realize that she was a lot smarter than we are today. She may not understand the complexities of the internet, but we are the fools who cannot even preserve our summer vegetables so we don't starve in the winter.

We must address the classic American attitude of individuality. Our culture, probably more than any other culture in the world, is based on the individual. Our economic system fuels this individuality. Look at our eating habits. Rather than supporting our community, we buy cheap food from far-away places in chain supermarkets. We do not realize what we are doing to our own community, because we no longer think about our community—we think only of ourselves. Eating can no longer be an individual act. It is not about whether an individual wants to get fat or die from gluttony.

Antibiotics are becoming less and less efficient as pathogens and virus mutate. It seems clear that this is directly related to the excessive use of antibiotics in our food supply. Roughly 75 percent of all antibiotics in this country are given to our livestock. Again, I am not a scientist, but it seems quite clear that even people who only eat antibiotic-free meats will find their medicine useless, as a mutated virus will resist antibiotic treatment regardless of what kind of meat was eaten. The use of pesticides can be equally harmful to the strict organic eater, as a personal choice at the dinner table can do nothing to stop the chemicals of conventional farms from seeping into the rivers and soil. We should all have a right to eat clean, healthy, and sustainable food. It should be a privilege to eat exotic and out-of-season food. Right now, however, we have the right to eat exotic and out-of-season food, and the privileged few can eat clean, healthy, and sustainable food.

When we fully realize or finally admit the effects of climate change, peak oil, and globalized food as our primary source of food, food from international sources will be more expensive than local food. How do we get back to where local food is normal and affordable, and food from far away is exotic and truly expensive? We have successfully wiped out most of the farms and do not have many farmers left. I can only hope that we can start supporting our local farmers-real support, not the tokenistic once in a while local treat. We must face the reality that urban sprawl must give way to farmland. We must realize that we cannot eat beef every day, but, at least when we do it won't kill us. This will involve spending more of our money, but soon the amount we spend on food will feel normal and not expensive. Americans pay less per capita than anyone else in the world for food.

It should be really easy for privileged people to buy fewer luxury items and spend the same percentage of income as other people in the world do on food, but the same cannot be said for the majority of people in the U.S. Most people in this country are dependent on their weekly wages and live paycheck to paycheck. Wages are set to allow people to survive so they can show up to work. There is little extra money put into that equation for clean, sustainable food.

We could hope that more farms will appear and there will be more 25 farmers to provide enough real food for everyone at an affordable price. We could hope that supermarkets and agro-business would just take care of the problem for us and magically make good, clean, fair, sustainable food cheap enough to fit into our current model. Or hope that these same businesspeople who have ruined our food supply and who are wrecking our land will take their millions of dollars of profit and happily give it back to the farmers and small producers-people who see food as sustenance, not commodity. But that just is not going to happen.

As our food entered our economic systems it was transformed from sustenance to commodity, and I do not see how we can take it back while maintaining this economic system. We have to ask ourselves what we want, food or our current economic system. We need to realize that our system itself is not sustainable and has failed.

[2007]

RICHARD DELGADO

Hate Cannot Be Tolerated

Educated at the University of Washington and the University of California–Berkeley, **Richard Delgado** is a leading commentator on race in the United States. His 1996 book *The Rodrigo Chronicles: Conversations about America and Race* was nominated for the Pulitzer Prize and won the Gustavus Myers Prize for outstanding book on human rights in North America. In addition, he has edited or authored five other books that have won the Gustavus Myers Prize, including the 1995 *The Price We Pay: The Case against Racist Speech, Hate Propaganda, and Pornography*, edited with Laura Lederer, and the 1996 *The Coming Race War? And Other Apocalyptic Tales of America after Affirmative Action and Welfare*, which also won the 1997 American Library Association Choice Outstanding Academic Book Award. Delgado is currently the University Distinguished Professor of Law and Derrick Bell Fellow at the University of Pittsburgh School of Law.

In his essay "Hate Cannot Be Tolerated," Delgado defends hate-speech codes that some colleges have recently enacted. Hate speech, he argues, does not foster conversation and is a veritable "slap in the face" to its victims; thus, rules that govern it should be applauded.

Anonymous vandals scrawl hate-filled graffiti outside a Jewish student center. Black students at a law school find unsigned fliers stuffed inside their lockers screaming that they do not belong there. At a third campus, a group of toughs hurls epithets at a young Latino student walking home late at night.

In response to a rising tide of such incidents, some colleges have enacted hate-speech codes or applied existing rules against individuals whose conduct interferes with the educational opportunities of others. Federal courts have extended "hostile environment" case law to schools that tolerate a climate of hate for women and students of color.

Despite the alarm these measures sometimes elicit, nothing is wrong with them. In each case, the usual and preferred response—"more speech"—is unavailable to the victim. With anonymous hate speech such as the flier or graffiti, the victim cannot talk back, for the hate speaker delivers the message in a cowardly fashion. And talking back to aggressors is rarely an option. Indeed, many hate crimes began just this way: The victim talked back—and paid with his life.

Hate speech is rarely an invitation to a conversation. More like a slap in the face, it reviles and silences. College counselors report that campuses where highly publicized incidents of hate speech have taken place show a decline in minority enrollment as students of color instead choose to attend schools where the environment is healthier.

A few federal courts have declared overly broad hate-speech codes 5 unconstitutional, as well they should. Nothing is gained by a rule so broad it could be construed as forbidding the discussion of controversial subjects such as evolution or affirmative action.

But this is not what most people mean by hate speech, nor are colleges barred from drafting narrow rules that hone in on the conduct they wish to control. And when they do, courts are very likely to find in their favor. Recent Supreme Court rulings striking down laws upholding affirmative action and approving punishment for cross-burning show that the court is not unaware of current trends. Society is becoming more diverse. Reasonable rules aimed at accommodating that diversity and regulating the conduct of bullies and bigots are to be applauded—not feared.